DAVE MULÉ

ACROSS THE SEAMS
Professional Baseball in
Jamestown, New York

ISBN 0-8488-2514-4

Amereon House,
the publishing division of
Amereon Ltd.
Post Office Box 1200
Mattituck, New York 11952-9500

Front Cover: *The Falcons at home in 1944. Nellie Fox (#11) is in center field.*

For Ann

*Celoron Park, the original home of professional baseball
in Jamestown.*

ACKNOWLEDGEMENTS

Across the Seams began with a meeting between Greg Peterson and Mike Billoni, general manager of Rich Baseball Operations. Their goal was deceptively simple: gather historical data about professional baseball in Jamestown between the years of 1939 and 1994, then funnel that material into a single text.

A research committee was created, consisting of Russ Diethrick, Greg Peterson, Mary Lou Scully, Emory Olson, Doug Sitler, Peter Norlander, Durwood Swanson, Bonnie Magers, Charley Burley Edwards, Robert Johnson, William O'Donnell, Lorraine Quattrone, Jim Riggs, Sam Teresi, Terry Heslink, Lyle Peterson, Paul Palisano, Chip Johnson, and Jim Wingett.

The research committee received 1941 archival footage from the family of G. William Samuelson. The James Prendergast Library and its staff made the reference desk exceedingly available and taught researchers how to use the microfilm machines. Lowell "Mickey" McKain of the Falconer Historical Society, members of the Celoron Historical Society, and Wendy Chadwick Case and Karen Livesay of the Fenton Historical Society provided photos, newspaper accounts, and other background material. Baseball historian Joe Overfield gave insight into the relationship between the Detroit Tigers, Buffalo Bisons, and Jamestown

Falcons. Many members of the community, too numerous to mention, provided old programs, pictures, scrap books, and newspaper articles.

Russ Diethrick and Greg Peterson instituted a "Hot Stove Luncheon" which brought special guests to Jamestown to relate their baseball memories. Those who participated include Vince McNamara, Flo Wick, Tony Phillips, Jackie Moore, Bob Kerr, Dave Werner, Jack Fulford, Mike Billoni, Ralph Mee, Tom Sharpe, Park Catchpole, Cy Williams, Dan Carnevale, Lyle Parkhurst, Bob Olson, Len Anderson, Dan Lunetta, Steve Johnson, John Pollock, Tom Hurst, Al Taylor, Orv Cott, John Jachym, Jack Gallagher, Phil Regan, Frank Heller, Russ Diethrick, Joe Nalbone, Charles Panebianco, Tom Weakley, Swat Erickson, Larry Parrish, Art Asquith, Bob Bastion, Stan Lundine, John O'Neil, Babe Birrer, Jerry Lawson, Gunnard Kindberg, John Venable, Theo Ganey, Jim Roselle, Tom O'Reilly, Jim Barone, Harry Martenson, Don Malmrose, Bob Brown, and Marian Rizzo.

Additional source material was provided by George Gmelch, Joe Ginsberg, Marquis Grissom, Jason Gibbons, Frank Bolling, George Lerchen, Tony Lupien, George Goodell, Robert Peterson, Todd Hundley, and Delino DeShields. Gracious assistance came from family members of players who played in Jamestown, including those of John Newman, Clem Koshorek, Ted Wybernac, Richard Schmidt, and Jerry Klein. Jim Riggs, current sports editor of the *Jamestown Post-Journal*, graciously made his baseball files available. Finally, Elizabeth Hyde—widow of long-time sports editor Frank Hyde—made available the extensive files and background material that she had retained from her husband's career.

Pete Hubbell of WJTN, Greg Maeier of WKSN, and Allan Hall of Paragon Cable were helpful in publicizing the project, which resulted in a substantial reaction from the community.

The Buffalo Bisons and Jamestown Jammers staff—notably, general manager Mike Ferguson—provided invaluable assistance. All-time rosters and balloting were provided by Craig Short and Jim Alexander at Sequoia Pacific. Charlie Wride provided a register of Jamestown baseball personnel who went on to the major leagues.

Once the manuscript was underway, Sig Gissler, William Holmes, Dave Kartch, Jon Moskin, Michael Giudice, and Joe Mattis each helped guide the narrative while Mark Alvarez, Bob Pytel, Gary Kelleher, and Roger Kahn gave me a road map to the publishing community.

Ann, Mom, Dad, and my entire family showed extraordinary patience through four years of working and waiting. Jed Clauss, Joanna Paulsen, and Judi Lynn Lake at Amereon, through their faith in Jamestown and in me, brought *Across the Seams* to fruition. Very special thanks go to Fred Wilpon, Alan Griffith, Richard Ohmann, and Tom O'Reilly, without whose help this book could never have become what it is.

I feel it is only right to distinguish the effort put forth by Russ Diethrick and Greg Peterson from that of anyone else's. Without Russ, there would simply be no professional baseball in Jamestown today. It is a fitting tribute that Jamestown's ballpark was recently renamed in his honor. Greg's dedication to his hometown and his attachment to baseball gives Jamestowners a strong chance of maintaining a minor-league club into the next century. I will always be grateful for the opportunity to tell their story.

PREFACE

   Baseball and Jamestown have each had long and rich traditions. Famed ornithologist Roger Tory Peterson, Lucille Ball, and Supreme Court Justice Robert H. Jackson (chief prosecutor at the Nuremberg trials) all claim local birthrights. Similarly, Sal Maglie, Nellie Fox, Frank Lary, Donn Clendennon, Dwight Evans, Cecil Cooper, Ben Oglivie, Larry Parish, Marquis Grissom, and Randy Johnson are among the more than 100 major-league baseball players who started their climb to the "big show" from Jamestown, New York.

   I first met David Mulé when he was a student at Wesleyan University. To research his senior project on minor league baseball, he was permitted to tag along with the Jamestown Expos for the summer. He not only obtained a feel for the rigors of the day-to-day operations of professional baseball, but also the rich heritage of baseball as an integral part of this community. He traveled with and learned about the players, managers, and staff. More importantly, he worked the stands to meet former professional players and the local fans who have stood steadfast through the good and the bad times. He thereby gained an understanding of a community which has supported professional baseball for more than half-century.

The title of this book, *Across the Seams*, is appropriate. Since the earliest recorded baseball activity in the Jamestown area, there have been individuals both on and off the field who have maintained the infrastructure necessary to sustain the sport on a professional level.

In this book, you will be introduced to the likes of Billy Webb, Ernest Kessler, Judge Allan Bargar, Russ Diethrick Jr., and others who have dedicated their time and talents, often without notice or fanfare, to assure the continuation of professional baseball in this area. This story is about those individuals: the managers who came as players and returned as leaders of Jamestown teams; the players, the staff, and, most importantly, the local fans who have continued their love affair with baseball.

Gregory L. Peterson
Jamestown, New York

ACROSS THE SEAMS

Part 1
O N E

CITY OFFICIALS, LOCAL BUSINESSMEN, THE Jamestown Falcons, and the visiting Batavia Clippers marched down the first base line and through the outfield grass into shallow center field. The American flag—red, white, and blue, with 48 stars—was raised on the center field pole as a bugler sounded the "Star Spangled Banner." When the anthem was over, Jamestown's mayor, Leon F. Roberts, stepped to a microphone behind the pitcher's mound and addressed the sell-out crowd.

"What we see here is not merely brick and mortar," Roberts said of the newly constructed Municipal Stadium. "It is not only a field enclosed with a fence. We see here today an enduring monument to the efficacy of civic enterprise."

"I welcome the Falcons to their new home," Roberts continued. "We hope it will be the scene of many triumphs. We give them our best wishes, and we give them our hearts. We pledge them our earnest support, and we know, in turn, they pledge to us their loyalty and their best efforts."

Jamestown, New York (pop. 35,775) is located in the southwest corner of New York State, 60 miles from Buffalo, 120 miles from Pittsburgh, and 140 miles from Cleveland. It is the birthplace of Lucille Ball and singer Natalie Merchant. At the turn of the century, Jamestown had the highest concentration of Swedes outside Sweden and was the second largest producer of fine furniture in the United States, behind Grand Rapids, Michigan. For much of its history, Jamestown has also had a professional baseball team.

It was Municipal Stadium that would provide the stage for many of the "triumphs" Mayor Roberts predicted, as well as the failures he surely anticipated. What none of the 4,200 fans at the stadium for the inaugural game could imagine were the stories that would unfold in the next 50 years as a result of minor-league baseball in Jamestown.

In March of 1939, representatives from Jamestown, Niagara Falls (N.Y.), Batavia (N.Y.), Olean (N.Y.), Hamilton (Ontario), and Bradford (Pa.) gathered in Buffalo to create the PONY (Pennsylvania-Ontario-New York) League. Jamestown's entry in the league was headed by *Jamestown Evening Journal* sports editor Stuart C. Maguire. Within two months, however, Maguire was overwhelmed by the financial and time pressures of running the local ballclub. On May 1, nine days before the season opener, Maguire resigned and transferred control of the team to a well-known Jamestown athletic official, William G. Broadhead.

Maguire, incidentally, would continue to chronicle Jamestown's baseball fortunes for three more seasons before leaving in 1942. He would go on to write for several newspapers before taking a job with the *Atlantic City Daily World*. Maguire, who drank heavily, died of a heart attack in October of 1946 in Atlantic City.

The Jockeys, as the team was called under Broadhead, opened up the 1939 season with six games on the road. The day before the home opener, Broadhead sold the Jockeys (which had won two and lost four) to the Pittsburgh Pirates to be operated as a farm team and named the Baby Bucs.

The Baby Bucs played at Celoron Park, five miles from downtown Jamestown, on Chautauqua Lake, in the middle of an amusement area. When it was built in 1893, Celoron Park was at the heart of the era's famous "Chautauquas," summer-time tent meetings where huge crowds gathered for educational lectures, concerts, and revivalist sermons. By the 1930s, the Celoron Park amusement area was known as the "Coney Island of the West," attracting top big-band musicians like Cab Calloway, Rudy Vallee, the Dorsey Brothers, and Guy Lombardo.

The highlight of the 1939 season came when the Pittsburgh Pirates visited Celoron Park for an exhibition game against the Baby Bucs, led by their manager, Pie Traynor, and their coach, Honus Wagner. Only 789 fans sat through a steady drizzle to watch the Baby Bucs' finest performance of the year, a 1-1 tie against the major-leaguers. Before the start of the seventh inning, play was stopped due to heavy rains and the Pirates left to catch their train to Boston to play the Braves.

Oddly enough, this was not Honus Wagner's first time at Celoron Park. In 1895, he played a significant portion of his first season in professional baseball against a short-lived Jamestown team called the Celorons. As members of the Warren (Pa.) Wonders, Wagner and his teammates dominated the Celorons all season long, arguably contributing to the ultimate collapse of the organization.

That summer, Wagner had already played 42 games with three other teams before coming to Warren in the middle of the season. When Wagner arrived, the Wonders were in fifth place, two games under .500. Four of Wagner's first eight games with Warren were against the Celorons; the Wonders lost the first game, then won the next three to jump-start their season. On July 29, Warren took over first place, passing the Wheeling (Pa.) Stogies (owned by Edward G. Barrow, future general manager of the New York Yankees from 1923 to 1939).

The Celorons, meanwhile, collected more errors than fans and saw greatness only vicariously through the teams that beat them. "The Jamestown people take a great deal more interest in balloon ascensions than they do in baseball," wrote a visiting reporter from Warren. Against the Stogies, the Celorons committed five errors, including a misplayed pop fly that resulted in two runs.

In mid-August, Wagner returned from an arm injury to help beat the Celorons and give the Wonders their 13th consecutive win. For the Celorons, it was their final loss. "Baseball Team Disbanded," the *Jamestown Evening Journal* mercifully proclaimed. "The Celoron Club Retires After a Brief and Disastrous Existence."

Unfortunately for Jamestown baseball fans, the 44 years between Wagner's appearances in the Jamestown area had not been kind to the Celoron Park ballfield. By 1939, as home to the Baby Bucs, the grandstand was wobbly and almost unusable, its roof was leaky, and changing facilities for the players were nonexistent. So while Baby Bucs' players and fans suffered through a 14-game losing streak in August that would send them to last place, the ballclub's future in Jamestown was tenuous. The Pittsburgh Pirates were pleased with the city of Jamestown but fed up with the team's playing facilities and were threatening to pull their players out of town if a new downtown ballpark wasn't built. Jamestowners needed to respond quickly with plans for a ballpark or lose their team.

The "Jamestown Citizens' Stadium Committee" was hastily formed to explore the proposition of building a new ballpark, an expensive and time-consuming effort that would require great resources and commitment. A lack of immediate results, however, convinced the Pirates that their energy and money would be better invested elsewhere. Two months after the 1939 season ended, the Pirates moved the Baby Bucs to London, Ontario and Jamestown was left without a team.

"No matter where the blame lies, a post-mortem isn't going to help matters for the present or the future," Maguire wrote in the early spring of 1940, when it became apparent that the PONY League would open without a Jamestown entry. "While loss of organized ball for a year is regrettable, it can't be helped, but things can be done to make a-bit-more-distant-future all the brighter for the local diamond cause."

At the start of the 1940 PONY League season, Jamestown didn't have a ballclub but they did have a Citizen's Stadium Committee run by two talented and focused Jamestown men named Ernest Kessler and Allan Bargar. Kessler was chairman of the committee. He was a thin man in his late 40s who was a leader in his community. In 1940 and 1941, Kessler focused the energy of Jamestowners towards the financing and construction of a new ballpark. "Ernie's Army"—Jamestown business executives, club members, and craftsmen—were on call like Minutemen.

Bargar, a town judge, was in charge of the Citizens' Stadium Committee financial campaign. In Jamestown, the name Bargar was synonymous with ethical standards. Eager businessmen, motivated by Kessler and convinced by Judge Bargar, comfortably wrote checks for the stadium cause.

Kessler and Judge Bargar's big break came when they heard of an "unfortunate" situation in Niagara Falls. Harry Bisgeier, owner of the PONY League Niagara Falls Rainbows, withstood anemic crowds in 1939, causing him to lose more than $15,000. The first month of the 1940 season was no more promising and Bisgeier was considering moving the Rapids to a town that could better support a minor-league baseball team.

"This is our chance," Kessler told his supporters. "We can get the franchise for the remainder of '40, but we still need a stadium in order to keep it." For $3,000, the stadium committee quickly purchased a 20-acre tract of land and turned the deed over to the city. Kessler and Judge Bargar hired the superintendent of Buffalo's Offermann Stadium, Joe Brown, to assist in the design process.

The promise of a new stadium was enough to convince Bisgeier to leave Niagara Falls. Midway through the 1940 season, Bisgeier moved his Rainbows to Jamestown.

The Falcons—a name selected from a fan vote which edged Mustangs, Orphans, and Allen Mitts—would play at Allen Park for the remainder of 1940, a temporary home until Municipal Stadium could be completed.

Allen Park was actually two diamonds on the south side of town used for semi-pro games. To prevent fans from watching games without paying, a burlap canvas was hung along the fence that bordered the park. A scoreboard was placed in right-center and temporary bleachers, borrowed from a local high school, were placed along the left and right field lines.

On July 19, 1940, the mid-season "opening day," a special bus service meandered through Jamestown to pick up anyone who wanted to see their new PONY League team play the Hamilton Red Wings. The Falcons lost the game 7-4 in front of 3,000 fans, placing them 15 games behind first place and five games out of fourth place, the final playoff position. But with a burst of energy, the Falcons reentered the playoff picture. In July, the Falcons won 14 out of 20 games to take over third place. Then, as quickly as the Falcons had revived themselves, they slipped again and lost seven of their next eight.

Bisgeier acted fast, securing Sal Maglie, an Italian-American pitcher from Niagara Falls. Olive complexioned with dark eyes and dark hair, Maglie was only 23 years old when he came to Jamestown.

"He's fast," commented the 1940 Falcons manager, Joe O'Rourke. "But he's hot and cold and doesn't appear to have a deep love for the game."

Maglie, not yet known as "The Barber" for his high-and-tight fastballs, would leave the Class D PONY League on a rise through the minors and finally into the major leagues with the Brooklyn Dodgers in 1945. Though Maglie had advanced, he remained unfocused. Between 1946 and 1949,

Maglie spent three seasons in the Mexican League, where he apparently developed a "love for the game."

In 1950, he returned to the major leagues, a more mature pitcher and person. That season, Maglie truly began a major-league career that would take him to all three New York City clubs of the 1950s—the Dodgers, Giants, and Yankees. "I suddenly realized baseball rewards you with what you put into it, just like anything else," Maglie said after he retired in 1958 with 119 wins and 62 losses.

The day Maglie arrived in Jamestown in 1940, the Falcons overcame a seven-run deficit to beat Bradford 8-7. The next day, Maglie pitched the first game of a doubleheader and went the distance, allowing only four hits and one run.

No one was more pleased to have Maglie than Jamestown's growing Italian community, which was introducing exotic foods like lasagna and ravioli to Jamestown's "Swede Hill." Maglie and two of his teammates were honored at a dinner by a group of Italian-American businessmen, who presented the players with traveling bags before a Falcons' home game against the London Pirates. The game was postponed because of rain, but Maglie pitched the next night and beat London 7-2 for a seven-hit complete game. With Maglie on the team, the Falcons were on a roll.

Heavy-set Falcons' left fielder John Newman was also contributing to his club's run at fourth place and the last playoff spot. In the second game of a doubleheader against Bradford, after defeating 19-year-old pitcher Warren Spahn, Newman demonstrated his power to Jamestown fans for the first time.

"The ball traveled on a line and was only 10 feet above the shortstop's head," Maguire wrote, "but in further transit, gained altitude. It wasn't a towering bash, but a line drive of tremendous velocity." Newman would hit many more home runs in Jamestown on his way to becoming a local legend.

On the last day of the season, with Jamestown in third place one-and-a-half games ahead of both Hamilton and

London, the Falcons were set to face the London Baby Bucs in a doubleheader. One win over London, or a loss by Hamilton, would secure a playoff spot for the Falcons. In the first game, London won on a pinch-hit single in the bottom of the ninth. Maglie started the second game but gave up five runs in the first. By the time an announcement was made that Hamilton had swept their doubleheader to leapfrog Jamestown and clinch third place, the Falcons were down 8-0. Now fighting head-to-head with London for fourth place, the Falcons regained their composure and scored seven times in the final five innings but still fell short. Jamestown's Falcons lost and finished fifth, one-half game out of a playoff spot.

During the off-season, Jamestowners came together behind Kessler and Judge Bargar. Checks, cash, and promises were given to Bargar, providing the Citizens' Stadium Committee with the necessary funds for the construction of the new ballpark. Bleachers were loaned to the city by the Board of Education, labor groups joined together to build the outfield fence, The Elks Club donated two flag staffs, and The Moose Lodge donated a scoreboard.

When the stadium was completed in March of 1941, Bargar Stadium was suggested as its name. "Why me?" the judge argued at a welcome dinner for the 1941 Falcons. "It belongs to the people. Just call it Municipal Stadium." He waved a finger at the Falcons' new manager, Greg Mulleavy. "You better win us a pennant, because that is the proper way to initiate a new stadium."

T W O

THE SILHOUETTES OF THE TWO MANAGERS GLOW-ed from the light of Municipal Stadium's lamps. Greg Mulleavy, the baby-faced manager of the Jamestown's Falcons, screamed into the little red face of Olean Oilers' manager Jake Pitler. Veins popped from both of their foreheads and the fans who surrounded them hollered and booed depending on their perception of the scene.

The home plate umpire separated the two managers and sent them back to their respective dugouts. Mulleavy's son, also the Falcons' bat boy, stood in the Falcons' dugout waiting for his father. When Mulleavy arrived, he leaned down to the visibly shaken boy and said, "Don't worry, son. It's not that serious."

"I would get so involved," recalled Greg Mulleavy Jr. more than 40 years later. "I thought it was for real and I used to get all upset. He never admitted to me that it was an act until much later."

Jake Pitler, Mulleavy's managerial rival, was a Russian-Polish Jew born in 1894 on New York City's Lower East Side. Pitler moved with his family to Pittsburgh as a young boy and grew up rooting for the Pirates, eventually working as a peanut-vendor at Forbes Field. He occasionally took fielding practice with the great Pittsburgh players of the time.

"[Hall of Fame shortstop Honus] Wagner gave me the best advice I had ever had," Pitler said. "'When you kick one, act as if you had caught it, and be ready for the next one. Never let it bother you, or you will miss the next one too.'"

Pitler decided to try playing baseball professionally and, in 1913, the Pirates signed him to a contract. Pitler worked his way through Pittsburgh's minor-league chain and made it back to Forbes Field in 1917, where he played 109 games for the Pirates at second base and shared the field with Wagner, who was in the final year of his playing career.

While the story of a peanut-vendor-turned-ballplayer was romantic, the dream was tainted for Pitler because the Pirates paid so poorly. Disillusioned, and with the short fuse that would later characterize his managerial style, Pitler "jumped" his contract for an attractive offer in Oil City, Pennsylvania and was suspended from organized baseball. To be reinstated, he would have to withdraw from organized baseball for one year and pay a $200 dollar fine. Pitler passed nine seasons in billiard rooms and ballfields, "turning a hand at whatever would make a buck," he later recalled.

By 1927, Pitler could no longer resist the lure of organized baseball. He scraped together $200 dollars, served his one-year suspension, and began his return the following season as a second baseman with a Binghamton, New York club. Pitler played, managed, and owned ballclubs on and off for the next decade, earning little and saving less.

"That's when I got my big break," he recalled later. "When all seemed gloomiest." Pitler was called upon by a business manager for a ballclub in Elmira, New York, one of the many acquaintances he had from his years of drifting.

Pitler was asked if he would be interested in the field manager position at Olean for the 1939 season. "Would I?" he answered. "I was on my way before I could hang up the phone." Pitler's Olean Oilers won the PONY League in 1939 and 1940, essentially unchallenged until 1941, Greg Mulleavy's first season as manager/second baseman for the Falcons.

Known as "The Whistle" because of his easily recognizable method of getting the attention of his players, Mulleavy was a natural leader, considered firm but fair by his players. "When Greg wanted to chew a player out he never embarrassed him," said John Pollock, his catcher in 1941. "He'd take you aside and let you have it—and invariably you had it coming."

Mulleavy was born in Detroit in 1905. He was 22 years old when he was discovered on a Detroit sandlot by a Chicago White Sox' scout. Mulleavy stayed in the upper minors, including eight years with the Buffalo Bisons, from 1927 until 1940. Harry Bisgeier saw him effectively handle young players in Buffalo and asked him to manage the 1941 Falcons. Mulleavy brought his wife and three sons with him to Jamestown.

Mulleavy's Falcons were known in the local sports pages as the "Mighty Mulleavians" and battled Pitler's Oilers throughout the summer. The Falcons remained in third place for much of the first month of the season, but scrapped their way into second in mid-July and finally jumped ahead of Olean and into first place in early August. No one did more to lift the Falcons into first than John Newman, playing his second season in Jamestown.

The legend of the 6-foot, 240-pound blond home-run slugger—the *Post-Journal* called him "The Sovereign of Swat," "Mastodon of Mace," "Blonde Bomber," "Baron of the Big Bingles," and "Swatsmith"—grew with each towering drive from his heavy bat. Children lined up to joke with the amiable, round Newman at parks from London, Ontario to Batavia, New York. He was the PONY League's Babe Ruth.

His natural ability to slug a ball could have led him to the majors; but in Minneapolis in 1937, with the baseball world at his young feet, Newman charged towards the second base bag, leaned his upper body back to the infield turf, and shot his legs forward in a fateful slide. His spikes caught on the rough turf and enough pressure was exerted to snap his left leg. Six months later, Newman had grown from 185 to 240 pounds in the hospital. A battle with obesity began that would cost him a chance at the major leagues and claim his life in Jamestown almost 30 years later.

Newman hobbled back to baseball and, three years after his injury, he became the most feared home run hitter in Owensboro, Kentucky. His charisma also made him a local celebrity. "The Steak House of the South," a restaurant in Owensboro, advertised the "John Newman Special." For 60 cents, one could order a small steak, creole sauce, candied yams, creamed corn, sliced tomatoes, hot rolls, and coffee, tea, or milk.

When the 1939 season ended, Newman was signed by Bisgeier to play for the Niagara Falls Rainbows in 1940, and soon became a Falcons' outfielder when the team moved to Jamestown.

Shortly after the Falcons claimed first place late in the summer, their clean-up hitter was celebrated at Municipal Stadium with a "John Newman Night." "Carefree and a bit of a clown on occasion," wrote Maguire in his column, "Roly Poly Johnny Newman came into his own last night as an honorary citizen of Jamestown." Newman was given a key to the city and made honorary mayor, police chief and fire chief of the town by Mayor Roberts. He was also presented a jar containing cash and coins, the result of a collection taken from the fans. His teammates gave him a defense bond.

"I sometimes try to joke a bit out there on the field, but tonight there's no room in my heart for that," said a tearful Newman into a microphone placed on the infield. "Mrs. Newman and I thank you, very sincerely." Newman added that he would like to remain a Jamestowner. Newman would get his wish; he would live the rest of his life in Jamestown, becoming a city bus driver when his baseball career ended.

In the first week of September 1941, the Falcons clinched their first PONY League pennant with a 14-4 win over Olean. The Falcons won their final three regular season games to streak into the semi-finals of the playoff against the Hamilton Red Wings.

The Falcons left Jamestown for Hamilton, Ontario in their two wood-paneled station wagons. Mulleavy drove across the Canadian border while his team shucked peanuts, leaving the shells to rattle on the dashboard. The station wagons and peanut shells would make four trips across Buffalo's Peace Bridge during the coming week and each crossing brought them closer to the end of a brilliant season. The Red Wings won the best-of-seven series in six games.

Harry Bisgeier immediately began preparations for the following season. Bisgeier and Joe Brown (designer of Municipal Stadium and scout for the Buffalo Bisons) traveled by train to Syracuse, New York and then to Jacksonville, Florida to scout and sign the 1942 Falcons.

Bisgeier, whose thin lips and narrow eyes made him look like he was always smiling, was born in New York City's Hell's Kitchen. As a young artist, he moved to Buffalo to design posters for the Shea Theaters. Eventually, Bisgeier drifted into the Buffalo sports scene, where his sharp sense of humor, natural gift for promotion, and ability to handle young athletes led him to purchase the Buffalo Bisons professional basketball team. Through his basketball experience, Bisgeier developed a relationship with the management of the Bisons baseball team. So when Bisgeier bought the Niagara Falls Rapids, he naturally turned to the Bisons for a working agreement.

Their arrangement was such that in exchange for the rights to any four Rapids' players, Bisgeier would have the inside track to sign players who didn't make the roster for the Bisons (who received their players from the Detroit

Tigers). When Bisgeier moved the Rapids to Jamestown, he linked the baseball fortunes of these four cities (Jamestown, Niagara Falls, Buffalo, and Detroit) for the first time in what would be a long and convoluted relationship.

"Giving Buffalo their pick of four men might deprive us of a tidy sum we could get for some salable player," said Bisgeier of the Falcons-Bisons-Tigers working agreement still in place for the 1942 season. "But the matter of assembling a winning team is paramount and means more to us than $5,000 or more for some star performer who would be sought by other clubs than the Bisons." Meanwhile, PONY League officials decided to play ball that summer despite the beginning of World War II, believing that baseball was essential to state-side morale.

As they had in 1941, the Falcons battled with the Olean Oilers throughout the season. The two teams quickly distanced themselves from the rest of the league. Their race for the pennant was made even more dramatic by having indirectly swapped two players: George Zimmerman and Duane Shaffer. George Zimmerman, a regular catcher for the Oilers in 1941, had "differences" with the Dodgers' management (which owned the Oilers' club) and was released. Bisgeier needed a backup catcher and bought Zimmerman's contract in the off-season. Raised in Western Pennsylvania, Zimmerman had spent two years working in a coal mine before catching the eye of a Pittsburgh scout while playing for a local semi-pro team. Tall, thin, with a rugged-lined face that made him look older than his 24 years, Zimmerman was expected by Bisgeier to be light-hitting but solid defensively behind the plate.

Duane Shaffer was with Maglie and Newman in 1940 when their Rainbows moved from Niagara Falls to Jamestown's Allen Park to become the Falcons. The right-handed pitcher from Oklahoma felt so comfortable in Jamestown that he moved there with his wife and started a family. Shaffer returned with Jamestown's pennant-winning club in 1941 and was signed by Bisgeier to pitch for the 1942 Falcons. Six feet tall, with an angular jaw and large ears, Shaffer began the season with the Falcons but, due to spotty health and a losing record, was released by Bisgeier. Shaffer was quickly picked up by Pitler's Oilers, who needed pitching for their 1942 stretch run against the Falcons.

During the first week of August, with their teams locked in a pennant race, Shaffer's Oilers came to Jamestown for a crucial doubleheader against Zimmerman's Falcons. More than 4,600 fans, men in dark suits and women in floral dresses, came out to the park. Those who couldn't be contained in the grandstand and bleachers pressed against the left and right field fences, literally bowing the chain-link barrier.

They saw the Falcons sweep Olean, putting the locals ahead by three-and-a-half games in the pennant race. With only two weeks remaining in the season, Mulleavy led the charge into Hornell (N.Y.), 60 miles east of Jamestown, to face the Pirates.

That night, second baseman/manager Mulleavy was spiked hard on his ankle while applying a tag at second base. Mulleavy stayed at his position throughout the game, placed a light bandage on the wound later that night, and kept the pain to himself until two days later, when a slide aggravated the unhealed injury. In Lockport, three days after being spiked, the swollen and red ankle became so unbearably painful that Mulleavy was unable to walk.

Bisgeier made arrangements with a doctor in Lockport for Mulleavy to receive medical attention prior to the Falcons' game that evening. Mulleavy was immediately admitted to the Lockport City Hospital with a badly infected ankle and forced to lie in bed while the Falcons took the field a few miles away. With John Newman as interim manager, the Falcons put on an eight-error display but came away with a win anyway over the shabby Pirates to remain three-and-a-half games in first. The next afternoon, Newman brought the Falcons to Mulleavy's room for a visit before making the trip back to Jamestown to continue the pennant drive. Bisgeier kept Mulleavy posted over the next three days while the Falcons dropped a doubleheader to Lockport and lost to Olean the next night to place them back in a tie with Pitler's Oilers. Mulleavy was released from his bed with less than a week remaining in the 1942 regular season and hobbled back to his spot at second base. Newman knocked a homer that night to take the second of a two-game set from Olean, giving back the Falcons a one game lead in the league standings. Newman's homer was his 30th of the season, one more than the PONY League record he set in 1941 and a mark that would remain intact for 12 years. The Falcons held off the Oilers with a doubleheader split in Olean and two more wins, to claim their second consecutive pennant.

In the semi-finals, the Falcons rocked Hornell in three straight games, outscoring them 24 runs to one, including two home runs by Newman in the second game. In the other semi-final match-up, between Olean and Bradford, Duane Shaffer threw a six-hitter for the Oilers in the opener; the Oilers went on to sweep the series. The Governors Cup champion would be decided by a best-of-seven series between Jamestown and Olean.

The excitement of the 1942 pennant race had only one precedent: the success and homecoming of Hugh Bedient. Bedient's baseball notoriety began in 1908, at 18 years old, when his semi-pro club faced a team from nearby Corry, Pennsylvania. On a surreal summer afternoon, Bedient cut the air with fastball after fastball that, after leaving his hand, seemed always to land in the soft leather target of the catcher's mitt. Batters and innings passed quickly, neither team managing a run until a throwing error in the top of the 23rd inning gave Bedient's team the win. When it was over, Hugh Bedient had struck out 42 Corry batters in a 23-inning complete game.

The feat shot through the newspaper wire services, prompting professional baseball clubs across the country to make immediate offers. Bedient signed a contract with the Boston Red Sox and hopped on a train heading east to show off his young arm in the minor leagues of New England. In 1912, his remarkable arm propelled him to the majors with the Red Sox. Bedient won 20 games that season, helping his team to reach the World Series against the New York Giants.

Bedient took his second turn of the Series at the mound in the fifth game, having already pitched one scoreless inning apiece in the second game and the third game (one of only three in World Series history to end in a tie). Bedient pitched through a low fog and kept John McGraw's Giants off balance with a slow ball he had developed in Jamestown. "It was a perfect day for me," Bedient said.

In Jamestown, a special play-by-play scoreboard was erected on a platform attached to the front of the Jamestown Post building on Washington Street. Scoreboard operators received information directly from Fenway Park over special press association wires, and thousands of Jamestowners followed the game from the streets below.

Bedient threw nine spectacular innings against the Giants, allowing just three hits and one run to beat New York (and their pitcher, Christy Mathewson) 2-1. Bedient would have had a shutout, but a Red Sox error allowed Fred Merkle to score the Giants' lone run in the seventh.

The Giants beat Bedient's Red Sox in the next two games to even the Series at three games apiece and force an eighth game in Boston. Bedient and Mathewson, for the second time in the Series, squared off. In Jamestown, fans again assembled on Washington Street to follow the game from the Post Building scoreboard. Bedient allowed just two runs in seven innings before being taken out for a pinch hitter in the bottom of the seventh.

Three innings later, the Red Sox won one of the most infamous World Series of all time, helped by the error of Giants center fielder Fred Snodgrass. In Jamestown, Hugh Bedient was an instant hero.

Bedient came home three days later and was greeted at

the train station in neighboring Falconer by 3,000 people, then in Jamestown by a parade of 25,000 more friends, relatives, and admirers. They welcomed him home, the biggest welcome ever for an area citizen. He and his wife were invited to an almost interminable array of parties, formal dinners, theater dates, and other public appearances. For more than a week, Bedient was the center of attention; every singer, instrument, and public speaker in Jamestown was made available to praise him.

"We have had a pleasant time since coming home," he said nervously at one of the many banquets that week. "We thank you for the interest you have shown. That is all I can say." Bedient sat down to a standing ovation that lasted five minutes.

In 1942, Jamestowners were in a fervor which eclipsed the innocent enthusiasm of the 1941 playoffs in its intensity and its breadth. Baseball was on the lips of everyone at downtown newsstands and hangouts like the Humidor and Gunhill-Carlson. "We're not going to let Jittery Jackie Pitler taunt us into such tantrums as might so upset our equanimity that we'd have to stay home in a rocker on the verandah," wrote Maguire in his column. The series opened with Olean winning 1-0 in 13 innings. Jamestown won game two by one run and game three, a rain-shortened contest in which Jamestown's starter retired the final 12 batters he faced, by a score of 1-0. The Oilers evened up the series in game four, taking advantage of walks and errors by the Mulleavians, but the Falcons hit their way to a game five decision 11-6 to give them the series lead three games to two, only one win away from a Governors Cup.

A cold drizzle fell before the sixth game at Olean's Bradner Stadium, a 45-minute drive east of Jamestown, and continued into the early innings as the heavy September clouds hung low. For eight and two-thirds innings, Olean's pitching kept the Falcons, and the small congregation of Jamestown fans who made the trip, in check. Olean's hitting punished Jamestown's pitchers for eight runs.

The score was 8-3 in the top of the ninth and the Falcons were down to their last out with a man on first. Many Olean fans stood in the exit ramps waiting for the final out, anticipating a seventh game in Jamestown. Newman then hit a double to give the Falcons a run and bring a few Oleanders back to their seats. A single followed to put another man on base for Mulleavy. His solid single up the middle brought Newman home to make it 8-5. Pitler called for Duane Shaffer, former Falcons' pitcher and current Jamestown resident, to come on to pitch in relief.

The next Falcons' hitter bashed a Shaffer pitch to drive in another run and cut the lead down to two runs. On the first pitch to the next batter, Mulleavy stole third to take the force play away from third base. With men on first and third, the batter was walked to load the bases for former Oilers' back-up catcher George Zimmerman.

Shaffer started Zimmerman off with two low curveballs but the Falcons' catcher wouldn't take the bat off his shoulder. The next curveball came sweeping across the strike zone and Zimmerman swung. The three runners bolted from their respective bases at the crack of the bat. Oilers' fans watched in horror as the scattered and outnumbered Jamestown fans leaned forward in their seats. The ball started low and fast, then rose higher and higher, and eventually passed over the right field wall to give the Falcons the lead, 9-8.

Duane Shaffer placed his hands on his hips, lowered his head, and walked around the mound. Oleanders cursed and Pitler paced deliberately in front of his dejected players. At home plate, the Falcons greeted Zimmerman, their newest hero, with smothering slaps and bear hugs. Attention only partially shifted back to the game, where Shaffer collected himself and retired the final man of the inning. The Oilers' hitters took their turns at bat but never mounted a real threat. The Jamestown Falcons won their first Governors Cup.

Falcons' fans transformed the cafes and bars of Olean into

a celebration, complete with toasts to Mulleavy, Newman, Zimmerman, Bisgeier, Kessler, and Bargar. Later that night, the Falcons rolled through the quiet and pitch-black residential streets of Jamestown in their station wagons, and into the parking lot of Municipal Stadium. A small gathering of Jamestowners were there, waiting for the team to arrive. They were eager to congratulate the Falcons and show their appreciation for professional baseball.

T H R E E

$\mathcal{H}$ARRY BISGEIER WAS CALLED TO WAR DUTY FIRST. Before he left, aware that teams and leagues were folding at an alarming rate, Bisgeier arranged for the St. Louis Cardinals to operate the Falcons in his absence.

"We believe we owe it to the game and to the morale of war industry to keep it going," Bisgeier commented before he left in the late fall of 1942. "Profits may be the exception," he added, "but we stand ready to make sacrifices." Three-quarters of all minor-league ballpark offices were cleaned out, and their stadium gates chained shut, between Zimmerman's grand slam and opening day of 1943. The Falcons and the PONY League marched on.

Soon after Bisgeier left, Newman was called by the Chicago draft board. "Baseball has been good to me," Newman commented from his Jamestown home. "I have had the breaks in baseball. I have received much more than a living from the game and I'm ready and anxious to serve my Uncle Sam wherever I am needed most."

The Falcons' new manager was Jack Sanford, a fiery Georgian who had managed the Batavia Clippers in 1939, 1940, and 1942. Early in the season, his biggest problem was pitching. "I have followed this game for 30 years and I have never heard of, nor seen, nor read of a pitching corps, not a man of whom can be depended on to locate the plate," Sanford said of his 1943 pitching staff. "I haven't a chucker who isn't liable to throw the ball clear over the grandstand at any given moment." Bob Vetter, a quiet right-hand submarine pitcher from Buffalo, was the lone exception to the Falcons' poor pitching and was scheduled to throw when they traveled to Batavia on June 16.

Because the Falcons' regular catcher was ill and their roster was already war-time thin, Sanford's team was without a backup catcher. Word passed that the stadium electrician and handyman, an Olean resident and father of five named Al Bermingham, was a respectable amateur catcher. Sanford was left with few options and Bermingham had already agreed to lend the visiting Falcons a hand, so he was signed to a one-game contract. Vetter skeptically took the mound, got the sign from Bermingham, and went into his side-arm delivery. Two hours later, Vetter had thrown the first Jamestown no-hitter in PONY League history and beaten the Clippers 9-0.

"He was a swell catcher," Vetter said of Bermingham, "and plenty smart back there. I took every sign he offered without shaking him off once." Four weeks later, with a 7-4 record, Vetter was called into service and left Jamestown.

Despite Vetter's no-hitter, Ernie "Solid Folks" Hrovatic was the Falcons' star. Women and men (who grew more scarce in Jamestown each week) walked down the streets of the town peppering their conversations with talk of Hrovatic and his line drives to deep left-center. The handsome, brown-eyed right fielder was regarded by the head of the St. Louis Cardinals' farm club system, Joe Mathes, as one of the greatest prospects he'd seen in 10 years. The summer progressed in war production and a Hrovatic-led batting order topped the league in hitting. Under the haze of July's and August's electricity-conserving day games, Hrovatic carried the club on his strong wrists and powerful shoulders. He also returned the admiration of Jamestowners, becoming increasingly taken with the warmth of their reception. Hrovatic led the league in hitting for much of the season until a slump near the end of the summer dropped him to second and triggered an eight-game losing streak for the Falcons. Still, the Falcons were good enough for fourth place and a playoff spot.

Hrovatic's Falcons surprised pennant-winning Lockport in the semi-finals, but baseball had to share the attention of Jamestowners with the war. In the finals, the Falcons took Wellsville (N.Y.) to a deciding seventh game at Municipal Stadium. The Falcons lost in front of a small crowd. Almost a year to the day that George Zimmerman had whirled Jamestowners into a frenzy, the war proved to be too much of a distraction. It was a disappointing end to the season, but wise fans knew they were fortunate to have had minor-league baseball at all in 1943.

Following the finals against Wellsville, Hrovatic left for his home in Salem, Oregon. During the fall, he was instructed by the Cardinals to report to their Pacific Coast League club, a short step to the majors, the next spring. Hrovatic visited his friends in Jamestown for Christmas and his future looked bright. But before he could report to the Pacific Coast League, Hrovatic was called to war service. He would make another visit to Jamestown in June, before being sent overseas later that summer, a visit that gave him a chance to watch a 1944 Falcons game at Municipal Stadium.

"If I come out of this thing all right, and if I go on to make the majors, I'm going to make Jamestown my home when I am done with baseball," he said during the visit. "I like the town and I like the spirit of the people, not only the baseball fans, but others whom I have met here."

Six months later, a phone call came from Oregon to a

friend of Hrovatic's in Jamestown. It was Hrovatic's mother calling to inform his friends in Jamestown that her son would not be returning. Hrovatic, an infantryman, had been killed on a German battlefield.

The 1944 season got off to a promising start when Harry Bisgeier returned, under the "38-year rule," from his Army tenure. In February, he reclaimed the Municipal Stadium lease and the Falcons, both of which Cardinals' management had hoped to retain but were obliged to relinquish.

Bisgeier's first task was to put together a strong pitching staff for his 1944 Falcons. A break came when "Lefty" Lyle Parkhurst, a Falcons' pitcher in 1942 and a Buffalo Bisons' pitcher under Mulleavy in 1943, came home to Jamestown to be the centerpiece of the Falcons' staff. Bisgeier's Buffalo-Detroit working agreement gave him the opportunity to pick up Parkhurst, who had a disappointing start with Buffalo losing three games in relief.

"I want to dispel any doubts that he came down to Jamestown from Buffalo because he didn't make good up there," said Bisgeier in defense of Parkhurst. "Parky was scheduled to go higher in baseball, but I asked him to come to Jamestown. He is 19 years old. If he works regularly, I feel he is definitely of big league caliber. He is destined to be a big-league pitcher in my book." Parkhurst's friends and family were happy just to see the slender southpaw, who had spent his youngest years hearing the story of how his father twice shaved Babe Ruth during a controversial barnstorming trip to Jamestown.

On the night of October 13, 1921, the day after the Yankees' lost the World Series to the New York Giants, reports circulated in the New York papers that Ruth and several other New York Yankees had signed contracts with a local promoter for a barnstorming trip, to start immediately after the last Series game. At the time, a trip of this nature was forbidden under the rules of baseball, and Major League Baseball Commissioner Kenesaw Mountain Landis called Ruth to warn him of the consequences. Ruth told Landis that he was catching a midnight train to Buffalo, where he would begin the first lap of his barnstorming trip.

"Oh you are! Are you? That's just fine," snapped Landis. "But if you do, it will be the sorriest thing you have ever done in baseball."

"Ah, tell the old guy to jump in a lake," Ruth said when Yankees owner, Jacob Ruppert, tried to prevent him from going. The stage was set for a battle as Ruth left for his dates in Buffalo, Elmira (N.Y.), Jamestown, Warren, and Scranton (Pa.).

The controversy stemmed from a rule which forbade players on World Series teams from appearing in exhibition games immediately after they played against each other. In the early years of the century, players from World Series teams often went on tours and reenacted the Series for local fans. Sometimes entire teams toured, though more often only two or three top players made the trip. The baseball establishment, fearing that the special impact of the World Series was being devalued, outlawed these games in 1911.

Ruth was aware of the rule, but because barnstorming was such a large portion of his income ($25,000 or more), he had asked Ruppert for permission. Ruppert agreed to allow Ruth and a few of his teammates, including Yankees' outfielder Bob Meusel, to make the tour if Landis consented. Landis held firm, determining that, even if the rule was unfair, it was part of the code of baseball. He vowed to enforce the rule and penalize those who violated it.

"I have warned Ruth that he need expect no light penalty if he appears in any further games this season," said Landis. Ruth, Meusel, and the rest of the "Babe Ruth All-Stars" ignored Landis' warning and played in Buffalo on October 14.

"Babe Ruth is Coming to City," the *Jamestown Evening Journal* headline read on October 17. "Stars defy Landis!"

"We are going to play exhibitions until November 1, and Judge Landis isn't going to stop us," said Ruth before his arrival in Jamestown. "I am not in any fight to see who is the greatest man in baseball. I am out to earn an honest dollar, and at the same time give baseball fans in these towns a chance to see the big players in action. I think we are doing something good for baseball. Why are we picked on while players from the second and third-place teams can play post-season games?"

Ruth strutted into Jamestown the night before the scheduled exhibition game at Celoron Park. He stirred a scene wherever he went, whether it was the stage where he spoke or just the Hotel Samuels' barbershop, where he was shaved twice by a barber named Stanley Parkhurst. "I'll never forget the day I had Ruth in my shop," Parkhurst recalled. "The street outside was jammed with people. They were peeking in the window and discussing The Babe." After his shave, Ruth spoke at the Winter Garden theater, warning young boys in the audience against the use of cigarettes and tobacco.

Rain fell throughout the day prior to the exhibition game but, during a long-distance hitting show, Ruth still hit a ball that sailed into Chautauqua Lake, a distance of over 500 feet. For the game, Hugh Bedient pitched for a local club that consisted of mostly semi-pro ballplayers from the Jamestown area. Bedient had been toiling in the minors since 1914, his final season in the majors with Ruth and the Red Sox. Bedient was hammered by Ruth and his All-Stars, allowing 20 hits and a homer by Meusel. Bedient's Jamestown team responded with 10 runs off of Meusel, who moved in from the outfield to pitch, to make the exhibition game a respectable 14-10 loss.

"I am going to take a turn at vaudeville for 16 weeks and I hope that Jamestown will be on my schedule," said Ruth after the game. He did give the stage a shot, but never again returned to Jamestown. After leaving Jamestown, Colonel Huston—a Yankees' co-owner along with Jacob Ruppert—met Ruth in Scranton. He found Ruth melancholy; the weather had been bad on the tour, therefore the crowds and the receipts were much lower than anticipated. Huston suggested Ruth end the tour and avoid the risk of Landis handing a year-long suspension to him and Meusel. Ruth agreed to pack it in and Huston paid off the local promoters.

Landis made his ruling in December. He withheld the World Series shares of the Yankees barnstormers and suspended them until May 20, 1922. Later, in view of the loss of part of their 1922 salaries, Landis paid Ruth and Meusel their withheld World Series shares. Landis also admitted later that the rule wasn't entirely fair and changed it so that players could participate in exhibitions up to October 31, provided that no more than three World Series players appeared in the same game.

Stanley Parkhurst, Ruth's Jamestown barber, stayed in Jamestown and remained one the area's biggest sports fans. His son, Lyle, combined his father's love for the game with an ability to pitch.

In 1939, at 14 years old, young Lyle Parkhurst would sneak into Baby Bucs games at Celoron. Before the booth where fans paid a 25 cents per car, Parkhurst would hop on the passengers' side running board of an unsuspecting fans' automobile and sneak into the park grounds. "I never paid for a ticket at Celoron," he said.

A 16-year-old high school student in 1941, Parkhurst sat in the grandstands of Municipal Stadium and watched the Falcons of Mulleavy, Newman, Zimmerman, and Shaffer run through practice drills. One afternoon, Mulleavy asked Parkhurst to toss batting practice. Parkhurst hopped up and took the mound, making himself ineligible for amateur baseball in Jamestown.

"We had an American Legion team in town, but they only played about five or six ballgames a summer," Parkhurst recalled. "You can do that inside of a week, and what are you going to do the rest of the summer."

The young southpaw continued to practice with the Falcons and began making road trips. After the season, Parkhurst (known also as "Parky" and "Lefty Lyle") went back to high school. In the spring, Bisgeier signed Parkhurst to his first professional contract for $65 a month.

In the summer of 1944, fans talked about Parky and the Falcons' chances against the first-place Lockport Cubs, managed by Greg Mulleavy, who took the Lockport job after spending the 1943 season managing the Buffalo Bisons.

Bisgeier and his Falcons' manager/left fielder Ollie Carnegie recognized the need for an outfielder who could also play the infield when needed. The hole was filled with Bisgeier's signing of 16-year-old Jacob Nelson "Nellie" Fox. "This kid will go on to the majors some day because he will just naturally fight his way up there," Bisgeier told Jamestown reporters.

Fox would go on to be a 12-time All-Star second baseman during his 19-year major-league career. His career highlights include playing 798 consecutive games at second base and winning the American League Most Valuable Player award in 1959 while leading the White Sox to their first pennant in 40 years. In 1997, Nellie Fox would become the first former Jamestown ballplayer to be elected to the Hall of Fame.

The excitement in the stands increased with each line drive by Fox, who hit .304 in 56 games for the Falcons. Jamestown fans, who needed a short respite from the long shifts in the war production plants of industrial Jamestown, followed from the stands and in the newspapers as their club held steady in third place for most of the summer.

One of the season's most dramatic moments came on August 9, when Mulleavy's first-place Lockport Cubs came to Municipal Stadium to face the Falcons. Parkhurst shut out the Cubs for five innings and took a 1-0 lead into the sixth, when he allowed two Cubs' runners to reach base, bringing Mulleavy to the plate. Parky threw the first pitch outside to his former Jamestown and Buffalo manager. Parkhurst tried to throw a fastball by Mulleavy on the second pitch but the Lockport manager pulled the ball hard. Manager Carnegie, playing left field, raced back to the fence but the ball cleared the wall, only the second home run Mulleavy ever hit at

Municipal Stadium. Despite two singles by Fox, the Cubs won the game and further solidified their lock on first place.

Jamestown's biggest local news that summer was that Lucille Ball, born and raised in Jamestown, filed for divorce from her husband, Cuban actor Desiderio Alberto Arnaz de Acha III, and said she was surprised their marriage had lasted four years. (Apparently their differences were at least temporarily resolved. Ball and Arnaz would not divorce until 1960.) "Me, I gave it a week," said Ball. Ball had appeared anything but divorce-bound during her visit to Jamestown nine months earlier, noted the *Post-Journal.* During her visit, Ball told reporters that Arnaz was the "No. 1 interest of her life" and that she hoped to co-star in a movie with him after the war.

Parkhurst, however, stole back the headlines on the final two nights of the PONY League season. On the second-to-last night, Parkhurst pitched a three-hit shutout on the road against the Erie Sailors, his 19th win and seventh shutout of 1944. The next night in Jamestown, he insisted to Carnegie that he again start against the Sailors. Parkhurst was given the nod and threw his second consecutive shutout, a five inning, rain-shortened game. His accomplishment—two shutouts in two days—received national attention in the sports press, gave Parkhurst his 20th win of the season, set a new PONY League record for shutouts (eight), and helped the Falcons edge the Batavia Clippers for second place.

The 1944 Falcons partially distracted Jamestowners from the war and incited the local fans to fill Municipal Stadium. After a semi-finals sweep of Batavia, Carnegie's Falcons' stunned Mulleavy's Cubs in the finals with Fox base hits and Parkhurst fastballs to sweep the series and win their second Governors Cup in three years.

That off-season, an old Dodge, filled to the roof with clothes and furniture, entered Jamestown driven by the *Post-Journal*'s new sports editor. "We rolled into Jamestown somewhat dubiously and were taken into the first house that had rooms for rent," he later recalled.

had rooms for rent," he later recalled.

Hyde was born near Jamestown, North Dakota in 1906. As a boy, he developed a fascination with the frontier which he maintained throughout his life. His grandmother, in fact, served breakfast to Jesse and Frank James after an 1871 bank robbery. She didn't realize who she had fed until a posse came by the next morning.

His first writing opportunity came as a 15-year-old copy boy in Yankton, South Dakota. Two friends offered him a ride to the Jack Dempsey-Tommy Gibbons heavyweight title fight in Shelby, Montana. A few days before the fight, Hyde was approached by a wire service reporter who asked if the teen-ager would be a "stringer" for the *Yankton Press and Dakotan* and provide highlight material to be added to the regular wire service story. Hyde accepted and phoned in his observations. One veteran reporter called Hyde the youngest man to ever cover a heavyweight title fight. Hyde was paid $3 for his contribution.

"I would have been glad to do it for nothing in exchange for a byline," he said.

During the Depression, regular jobs were scarce. Hyde spent a few days as a railroad section worker in North Dakota and became fascinated with telegraphy. With the aid of a night operator, he learned Morse code and was assigned a relief role on a section of track in Montana. He later took a job as a timekeeper and part-time motorman at a Butte, Montana copper mine. Then Hyde joined thousands of others "chasing the crops"—haying in Iowa, harvesting grain in Kansas, and picking apples in Oregon and Washington.

He spent one summer with Henry Kohlin's wrestling show on the carnival circuit. Having some high school wrestling experience, Hyde became part of a team that met all challengers in the ring. Anyone who dared would be paid one dollar for each minute he lasted with one of Kohlin's wrestlers.

"Those hometown men, framers, ditch diggers, construction workers and cowboys were usually noted for their ability in their area," Hyde described. "They came up with blood in their eyes." After the carnival, he settled in Glendive, Montana and took a job managing a billiard parlor and promoted boxing and wrestling cards.

Hyde was married in Glendive and soon moved to Billings, Montana with his wife, where he took a newspaper job, then on to the *Salt Lake City Tribune*, and, finally, to Jamestown in 1945. For the next 50 years, Hyde would chronicle professional baseball in Jamestown.

When the 1945 PONY League season began, Hyde was becoming acquainted with his new home and Allied prospects in World War II were becoming brighter. The Falcons opened their season in Erie with a moment of silence for the late President Franklin Delano Roosevelt after a flag-raising ceremony. On May 7, the *Post-Journal* read, "Germany Surrenders War in Europe" and Washington Street filled with celebrating Jamestowners.

The Falcons were in second place after one month of play. Their manager/shortstop, a former St. Louis Browns' shortstop named Jim Levey, was on his way to a .307 hitting season—an average helped by his still-blazing speed. (John McGraw once ranked Levey as one of the five fastest shortstops of all-time. During a marine track meet, Levey ran the 100-yard dash in 9.4 seconds, only one-fifth of a second behind Charlie Paddock's world record at the time.)

Overshadowing Levey's presence in the summer of 1945, however, was the return of Bob Vetter (who threw a no-hitter to a last-minute replacement catcher in 1943) to Jamestown. The story of Vetter's war experience and return to the Falcons was Hyde's first feature on a Jamestown baseball player. After the 1943 season, Vetter was drafted along with Ernie Hrovatic and dozens of other ex-Falcons. In July of 1945, three days after D-Day, Vetter stepped into the little French town of St. Lô where he and his platoon were caught in a German ambush.

"My whole face was paralyzed," Vetter told Hyde. "But I

sensed being hit several times. Shells were nicking the trees and it was fascinating to lie there on your shoulder blades and watch them. A burst would come over, sending down a little cascade of clipped leaves and wood splinters." Vetter and two others were discovered by a Red Cross worker and transported to a temporary hospital in a nearby hedge grove. Vetter entered a series of English convalescence units where he would slowly and steadily recover.

Vetter was honorably discharged in November of 1944, taking home a sustainer plate in his skull and a semi-paralyzed left arm, hand, and side. Against the odds, Vetter started a fight back to the pitchers mound. He notified the Cardinals' management, who still reserved his baseball rights, that he was ready to come back to baseball. They were amazed by his progress in spring training and assigned him to their Carolina League club.

Harry Bisgeier then bought Vetter's contract from the Cardinals and asked him to report immediately to Jamestown. "Bisgeier had a lot of faith in me," Vetter told Hyde when he arrived. "He taught me to have faith in myself. It's a long way and I've got a lot to learn, but now I am sure I'll make it."

In mid-June, Vetter walked out to the mound at Municipal Stadium, dropped into his submarine delivery, and fired a fastball to the plate. Vetter would finish the 1945 season with a 10-9 record and 14 complete games.

These were the stories that Frank Hyde told to Jamestown. He provided a layer of journalism that went far beyond box scores and preserved the history of Jamestown baseball as it happened. Hyde also understood the importance of homegrown personalities to Jamestown. Though not a Jamestown native, he immediately picked up on the stories of local interest, including that of "Two Shutout" Parkhurst.

Soon after Vetter's return came that of Parkhurst, who had been given another opportunity to pitch for the

The pennant winning "Jamestowns" of 1890-Jamestown's first professional baseball team, featuring R.A. Kelley at first base.

Hugh Bedient as a member of the Boston Red Sox.

Eric "Swat" Erickson, following his "miraculous" lemon peel-induced recovery, as a pitcher for the Detroit Tigers.

Ray Caldwell with Bob Feller-27 years apart, both no-hit the
Yankees as pitchers with the Cleveland Indians.

Celoron Park

Harry Bisgeier moved his Niagara Falls Rainbows to Jamestown in 1940 and changed their name to the Falcons.

Johnny Newman taking a swing in 1940 at Allen Park, the Falcons'
temporary home before the construction of Municipal Stadium.

Johnny Newman before a game at Municipal Stadium in 1941.

Buffalo Bisons after his remarkable performance with the Falcons in 1944. Parkhurst began the 1944 season with only two wins in eight decisions as a Bison; scouts and his managers attributed his ineffectiveness to his slight build, which limited his strength and endurance in the higher classifications of the minor leagues. On June 28, Parkhurst came home again to Jamestown to dominate the PONY League. He would complete all 15 games he started with the Falcons and win 11 decisions.

The 1945 Falcons won 19 out of 21 games at home, and 33 out of 39, beginning with Vetter's first start of the season. With the war still dragging on, however, even Vetter's and Parkhurst's returns could not sustain the level of enthusiasm that the Falcons had generated the previous August and September.

In mid-July, Umpire Charles Ross Badger made history at Municipal Stadium by becoming the first umpire to be married at the ballpark. "I have caught more Hades at home plate than most baseball men," said Badger, "so I wanted to be married right there and see if it would start a more lasting war."

The Jamestown Falcons and the Batavia Clippers marched slowly from their dugouts in single file. Their bats were slung over their shoulders as they fell into two lines to form an "aisle." Fans rang cowbells as the bridal party marched to home plate, where a minister awaited their arrival. After vows were exchanged, a nervous Badger forgot to kiss the bride, prompting fans to howl. "Badger came through in fine style," wrote Hyde of Badger's eventual kiss, "but so quickly his bride was caught unprepared and did not have a chance to lift her veil."

After the ceremony, the groom hurried off to change into his umpire's uniform while his bride, Lucy Badger, watched the ballgame from the grandstand. A collection was taken for the couple during the game which garnered $200, a safety pin, five pennies, one peppermint Lifesaver, six bus tokens, six red meat war-ration stamps, and a white button.

On August 6 and 8, two atomic bombs were dropped on Japan. Jamestown's relief that the war was over quickly turned to a restless desire to see their long-absent friends and relatives. The Falcons of Levey, Vetter, and Parkhurst finished in third, behind Mulleavy's second-place Lockport Cubs. The Falcons and Cubs again faced each other in the playoffs, this time in the semi-finals. Lockport won three out of four and went on to win the Governors Cup finals.

After the season, Mulleavy returned to his job in the men's clothing section of Bigelow's department store in Jamestown. Others who remained in town included John Newman, Duane Shaffer, Lyle Parkhurst, and Harry Bisgeier.

Most important was that Jamestown and the PONY League did what many towns and leagues could not do during World War II; they never stopped playing baseball.

F O U R

$\mathscr{A}$FTER FOUR-AND-A-HALF YEARS IN JAMESTOWN, Harry Bisgeier sold the Falcons to a 28-year-old businessman named John Jachym in 1945. Jachym would own, operate, and continue Bisgeier's success in making the Falcons the kings of the PONY League in attendance and in the standings for the next three seasons.

Jachym graduated the University of Missouri in 1940 with a degree in journalism and took a job with the Associated Press in Jefferson City. Before long, Jachym—who had played a few years of college baseball—was assigned to interview Branch Rickey, the general manager of the St. Louis Cardinals at the time. Rickey kept in touch with Jachym and, in 1944, asked him to join the Brooklyn Dodgers' front office. Unfortunately for Jachym, war service intervened.

When he returned from the Marines, Jachym looked for a job as a reporter in Western New York. By coincidence, he was offered a job with the *Post-Journal* for $12 a week, but a paper in Dunkirk (20 miles north of Jamestown) offered $15 a week so he took that job instead. In addition to reporting, Jachym took a part-time job as a scout for the Cardinals' organization. He would write until 2 p.m., when the paper went to press, then scout from 2 p.m. until 11 p.m. During this time, he often came into contact with Bisgeier and the Jamestown Falcons.

Rickey's son, Branch Rickey Jr., was also a bright and intuitive baseball mind who sensed Jachym's entrepreneurial capacity. "Knowing you, I think you'd be happier if you had your own ballclub," he said to Jachym.

"I don't have any money," Jachym answered.

"You'll raise it," Rickey Jr. replied.

By the time news of V-J day swept through Jamestown in August of 1945, Jachym had bought the team for $22,000 dollars, the highest price paid for a Class D yet. Jachym's parents gave him $2,000, he had saved about $5,000 more, and he borrowed the rest. One of Jachym's earliest team-related purchases was a 28-passenger converted school bus, which cost $2,000, to replace the old wood-paneled station wagons still used since the days of Mulleavy.

Bisgeier moved back to Buffalo. In 1955, he would help convince Buffalo baseball fans that they should buy the Bisons from the Detroit Tigers. Eager supporters purchased $150,000 in one dollar shares and bought the Bisons that fall. During the community's first four years of ownership, Bisons' stock paid its first dividend; they were among the most successful years in Buffalo baseball history.

In the fall of 1945, Jachym signed a working agreement with the Bisons and Tigers similar to the one negotiated in 1939 by Bisgeier. With his scout's instincts, Jachym searched for, and found, the best talent available. But Jachym still didn't have a manager in January and the 1946 season was fast approaching. Jamestowners knew who they wanted: their neighbor, and beloved former manager, Greg Mulleavy.

Speculations grew in Hyde's columns, in cafeterias, and in

the men's department of Bigelow's (where Mulleavy was kept as assistant manager more for his local popularity than for his marketing or fashion skills). Jachym decided not to hire Mulleavy. "If I let Greg Mulleavy manage the ballclub," he reasoned, "the next thing, the public is going to tell me who to pitch." He called up Mulleavy and explained the situation. Then Jachym called Branch Rickey in Brooklyn and asked if there were any positions available for Mulleavy in the Dodgers' system. The Olean position had not yet been filled and Mulleavy was given Jake Pitler's old job. Mulleavy would remain a Dodger, as would Pitler, until he died.

With Mulleavy in Olean, Jachym chose Marv Olson to manage the Falcons. A Swede and a former Bisons star, Olson was a popular choice in Jamestown. Known as "Sparky" with the Bisons, Olson was described by Hyde as "a strange sort of a cuss in one respect—he never says much but is still a 'driver.'" A conservative field manager, Olson played in the majors with the Red Sox in 1931 and 1932.

The day before the 1946 home opener, Major League Baseball Commissioner A. B. "Happy" Chandler stood at the podium of the Jamestown Wolf Club meeting hall. Sitting on a raised platform next to Chandler was Jamestown baseball hero Hugh Bedient and Tris Speaker, Bedient's teammate on the 1912 World Series champion Red Sox.

"If 'stubble patch' baseball—the baseball that is played in the alleys, back lots and corn fields of the nation—is permitted to die, then baseball will die all the way to the top," preached Chandler, the former Kentucky senator who took office as commissioner in April, 1945. Judge Kenesaw Mountain Landis, his predecessor and Babe Ruth's barnstorming foe, died in November of 1944 after 24 years in office.

As Chandler spoke in Jamestown, Cleveland Indians' pitcher Bob Feller was throwing a no-hitter against the New York Yankees in Ohio. It was the first no-hitter pitched against the Yankees since Ray Caldwell, another Cleveland

Indian, accomplished the feat in 1919. Caldwell happened to be sitting in the Jamestown Wolf Club with Bedient and Speaker that afternoon listening to Commissioner Chandler speak.

Born in 1888, Caldwell grew up in Corydon, a quiet community in the Jamestown area. Caldwell's first year in the majors was 1910 with the New York Highlanders, a team that changed their name to the Yankees in 1913 and shared the Polo Grounds with John McGraw's New York Giants. Caldwell, nicknamed "Slim" for his narrow face and build, pitched with the Highlanders and the Yankees from 1910 to 1919. From 1911 to 1915, Caldwell's club won 322 and lost 439. During those losing seasons, Caldwell (49 wins 47 losses) was one of the team's few winning pitchers. "Give Ray Caldwell a winning ballclub behind him and he would go down as one of the greatest pitchers of all time," said Hall of Fame manager Connie Mack.

Caldwell, whose love for baseball was unfortunately exceeded by his love for a drink, once pitched 49 innings over a six-game span before the Highlanders scored a run; he made that run stand up for a 1-0 decision over Detroit. Caldwell could also hit, and when he wasn't pitching he often played the outfield. He's the only pitcher to hit home runs on three successive days. "Yes, I had my moments," said Caldwell after he retired.

Caldwell was traded away by the Yankees to the Boston Red Sox in 1919 and would always feel hostility toward his old club. He played with the Red Sox for the first half of 1919, then was traded to the Cleveland Indians midway through that same season. In Cleveland, he received an opportunity to vent his anger.

Soon after his trade to Cleveland, the Indians faced the Yankees at the Polo Grounds. "Let me pitch against these guys today," Caldwell said to his manager, Tris Speaker (the same Tris Speaker who played with Bedient on the 1912 Red Sox). Though it wasn't Caldwell's day in the rotation,

Speaker sent Caldwell out to the mound. Caldwell hurled a no-hit, no-run game. A few weeks later, the Indians again made the trip east to New York and Caldwell again asked to take the mound. This time Speaker denied his request. But Caldwell got his chance to pay back his former club when Speaker put him into the game as a pinch runner in the ninth inning. Slim stole home for the only run of the game to beat the Yankees 1-0.

His first start with the Indians, however, was his most memorable game. It was the bottom of the ninth inning and Caldwell was on the mound in Cleveland with a 2-1 lead. Thick, dark clouds hung over the park. Suddenly, a bolt of lightning struck the field. The electrical current jumped to the players' metal cleats and through their bodies. The rest of the electricity dispersed into the grandstand. A stunned silence followed as about half of the crowd received a mild shock. All eyes turned back to the field where Caldwell was stretched out on the mound. In the confusion, the ball ended up in the hands of the Indians' shortstop Chapman who, along with Caldwell, received the worst shock. Caldwell staggered to his feet unassisted as did the shortstop, Ray Chapman. "Give me that danged ball and turn me toward the plate," Caldwell barked at his shortstop. Chapman handed the ball to Caldwell, who wobbled to the mound and peered into the catcher's mitt. The crowd hung on Caldwell's every move. Rain began to pour as Caldwell stood in his set position, then delivered the pitch. The batter topped a grounder to the second baseman, who tossed the ball gently to first to end the game, sending players and fans into the tunnels of the stadium to dry off.

A side note of Caldwell's story is that Ray Chapman, the Indians' shortstop who was also struck by lightning, was hit in the head by a Carl Mays' pitched ball and killed in mid-August of 1920. Following Chapman's death, the only one of its kind in major-league history, the Indians won the pennant. Caldwell won 20 games that season and started the second game of the best-of-nine World Series against the Brooklyn Robins. Caldwell retired just one batter, giving up two hits, a walk, and one run before being taken out of the game; his career post-season ERA stands at 27.00. Still, the Indians beat the Robins five games to two.

Caldwell stayed with Cleveland in 1921, where he finished his major-league career with a lifetime record of 133 wins and 120 losses, then returned to the Jamestown area where he would stay for the rest of his life. He never received a celebration like Bedient's, but Ray Caldwell would always be remembered, in the words of Frank Hyde, as "one of the greatest baseball personalities to ever don a uniform."

In 1946, Happy Chandler stayed in Jamestown after his speech at the Wolf Club for opening day the next afternoon. Two rows of city officials and color guard marched to Municipal Stadium's home plate, where the American flag was presented to the accompaniment of "The Star Spangled Banner." Three lines of fans waiting to buy tickets began at the stadium turnstiles. The lines extended back to Falconer Street at diagonal lines, then joined the road for more than a hundred yards. The war was over and Jamestowners were excited to see their Falcons.

Chandler, round-faced and wide-smiling, walked onto the field of Municipal Stadium to face the 5,162 Jamestowners who formed the largest opening day crowd in the eight years of PONY League baseball in Jamestown. "We owe gratitude to God that we are safely through the war ordeal," he said. "And we should dedicate this baseball season to the memory of those who died and those so crippled they will never play baseball again."

When Chandler concluded his speech, he returned to the first row of the grandstand. Next to Chandler sat the Falcons' new owner, John Jachym, who looked out at the club he had assembled. More than three-quarters of the Falcons had returned from war service, including Jachym himself, who had received the Silver Star and a Presidential Citation for his role in the battle of Guadalcanal.

On the field, Olson's Falcons hosted the visiting Hamilton Cardinals and their manager John Newman, Jamestown's former "Swatsmith." Following the 1942 season with the Falcons, Newman was drafted and served with a tank unit in the South Pacific. When he was discharged, Newman reported to Columbus, Ohio of the American Association. Columbus management gave him the choice of playing and managing in Duluth (Minnesota), St. Joseph (Missouri), or Hamilton (Ontario). He chose Hamilton to be near Jamestown, his adopted city. After managing the Hamilton Cardinals in 1946 and 1947, he would settle in Jamestown for good with his wife, Myrtle. "I always told my mother I'd play ball until I found a town I liked," he said. "I've found it—Jamestown."

Olson's Falcons beat Newman's Cardinals on opening day, and kept on winning early that summer. A strong pitching staff wracked up victories throwing to 25-year-old catcher Russ Kerns. Kerns had the dubious distinction of playing for a Class D team—the lowest rung in the organized baseball ladder at the time—the year after being a member of the World Series champion Detroit Tigers. In the war-depleted major-league season of 1945, Kerns was a backup catcher for the Tigers when they defeated the Chicago Cubs in the Series but was sent to the 1946 Falcons to develop the young players on Jachym's team. "Things broke in reverse for me once the shooting was over," said Kerns. "Maybe I can do a lot of youngsters starting out some good." Known as "Dick Tracy" since he tracked down a carnival worker who stole a suitcase from his hotel room, the blond catcher from Ohio would never make it up to the majors again.

Midway through the 1946 season, key injuries forced Jachym to sign a replacement infielder. Five-foot 2-inch Clem Koshorek, who had earned the Bronze Star for valor in an armored artillery division in Germany, was that infielder.

Stocky and square-jawed, Koshorek was sent in for his

first at-bat as a pinch hitter early in the summer. Municipal Stadium announcer Thore Carlson introduced Koshorek as "a new player from Royal Oak, Michigan." Above the din in the bleachers, a fan yelled, "Gee, he's a little squirt!" Koshorek swung, grounded out to short, and was thrown out by five feet, prompting another shout: "They can send him back to Royal Oak, wherever that is!" The next day, the Falcons were in Hornell and Koshorek was placed at third. Olson, normally the Falcons' third baseman, filled in behind the plate to give Kerns a rest. Koshorek fielded well and drove in two runs—the first tied the game at 4-4 and the second scored the winning run. He was soon moved to shortstop and nicknamed "Scooter" by Jamestown fans. Koshorek, who hit .299 for the season, became one of the most popular Falcons and (with Falcons' second baseman, Al Federoff) set a PONY League record for double plays. That summer, Jachym introduced Koshorek to Marilyn Cheney, a local girl and an employee of the Falcons. Koshorek and Cheney would marry in 1949.

Following the 1946 season, Koshorek moved up the Tigers' baseball chain and, after the 1951 season, played winter ball in Panama. While in Panama, he was released by the Tigers and picked up by the Pittsburgh Pirates, general managed by Branch Rickey. Jachym got word of Koshorek's move and was the first to call and tell him the news.

When Koshorek returned, he reported to Pittsburgh's spring training camp and was relegated to the Pirates B team, meaning he was not placed on the list of players who were to travel to their first pre-season series. Rickey called Koshorek into his office and told Koshorek, "We drafted you, but we know you can't hit, run, or throw." "What did you draft me for?" Koshorek answered. "I'll tell you one thing, Mr. Rickey, you give me a shot and I'm going to have the shortstop job on this club." There was a pause. "I think we've had enough conversation," Rickey finally said. "You go downstairs and I'll see you later on." When Koshorek arrived back in the locker room his name was on the list. He threw his bag together and rushed to join his teammates on their road-trip.

Koshorek played in the majors for two seasons with the Pirates, in 1952 and 1953. He hit .261 in 98 games in 1952. "I won't say he is the best shortstop the Pirates ever had," said Pie Traynor, "but they never had one with more guts."

Koshorek's guts placed him on the 1946 PONY League All-Star team—along with the man Jachym passed up for the Falcons' managing job, Olean manager Greg Mulleavy. Marv Olson and Russel Kerns, also All-Stars in 1946, helped the Falcons keep pace with the Batavia Clippers. Batavia and Jamestown finished the 126-game season tied for first. One more game would have to be played to break the tie.

League President Bob Stedler checked the PONY bylaws; there was no precedent and no specific mention of whether a one-game playoff would determine the pennant or simply playoff position. The question for those involved was whether both clubs would be declared co-pennant winners or was the one-game playoff also for the pennant. "The co-championship talk is only a rumor," said Stedler to Hyde. "As far as I am concerned, tonight's game is for the pennant." The *Post-Journal*, *Olean Times-Herald*, *Bradford Era*, and Jamestown radio station WJTN also endorsed the game.

On September 4, 1946, almost 6,000 fans came to Municipal Stadium for the one-game playoff against Batavia. With Stedler in the stands, Koshorek, Kerns, and Olson took the field for Jachym and all of Jamestown. Three runs in the first, two off of a Kerns' single, were enough to satiate the frenzied crowd. The Falcons beat the Clippers 6-2. Following the game, Stedler quietly mentioned that the league's board of directors would still have to make a ruling as to whether the game was for the pennant at their November meeting.

Jamestown won a best-of-seven semi-final series over Bradford to face Batavia again in the finals. The Falcons grabbed the opener 4-3 on a two-run single by Koshorek, a bouncer over the shortstop's glove. From there on, it was almost all Batavia and the Falcons lost the series, four games to two. Batavia celebrated again two months later when the league directors declared that the one-game playoff only determined first and second place in preparation for the playoffs, not the pennant. Therefore, the Falcons and the Clippers were declared 1946 co-pennant winners.

In 1947, Olson was again at the helm of Jamestown's club. By the Fourth of July, two returning veterans were leading the Falcons on the field: Kerns and first baseman Andrew "Doc" Alexson. A likable Greek left-handed first baseman, Alexson was with the Falcons in 1946 as Andrew Alexopolous before Americanizing his name in the off-season. At first base, Hyde wrote that Alexson "stretches like a pre-war rubber band and makes stops from the split position." At the plate, Alexson was strong in 1946 and devastating in 1947, winning the league batting title with a .338 average.

On July 3, the Falcons capped a streak in which they won 15 of 16 games. Mulleavy's Olean Oilers and Newman's Hamilton Cardinals fell like high school clubs, a seemingly inappropriate way for both managers to be making what would be their farewell appearances in PONY League uniforms at Municipal Stadium.

Newman's final stop at Jamestown's ballpark as manager of the Cardinals came in mid-August, for what would be another Falcons victory. When he stepped off the Cardinals' bus, he was swarmed by dozens of children begging for the job of batboy. "I'll be your batboy for nothing just to see the game!" one boy cried. Newman grabbed his bat bag and emptied its contents on the ground. "Heck, we'll all see the game," he said. "Now, each one of you fellows grab a bat and follow me." The children formed a line behind him and walked through the front gate where they were met by a questioning glance from a Falcons' employee. "You know how it is," said Newman without stopping. "No equipment, no game."

When the carnage of the regular season came to a close, the Falcons won the PONY League by 18 games. In the semi-finals, the Falcons disposed of Wellsville in five games. Mulleavy's Oilers also won their semi-final series in five games to set the stage for a battle between Olson and Mulleavy, Jachym's two former candidates for the 1946 managerial position and the two most significant Falcons' managers of the decade.

The Falcons won the first three out of four from the Oilers. The fifth game, a Saturday night which would be Mulleavy's last at Municipal Stadium, was won by the Oilers 3-2 to set up a game six at Olean. Mulleavy's last appearance in a Governors Cup game six at Bradner Stadium was in 1942, a night which ended with a George Zimmerman grand slam and the Falcons' first league championship. Five years later, Mulleavy no longer played the field and drama was not a defining characteristic of the game. The Falcons scored nine in the second inning, including a Kerns' three-run homer. The Falcons' right fielder, Ted Bartz, racked up seven RBIs and Doc Alexson added three hits and two RBIs. Olson's Falcons thrashed Mulleavy's Oilers 21-4 in front of a sickened Olean crowd. More than 500 Jamestown fans began the game in the bleachers blissfully razzing the full house of Olean fans as their club set a record for most runs scored in a playoff game. As the hits mounted, however, even the Jamestowners grew tired. The Falcons won their third Governors Cup and John Jachym was presented with the trophy. The Falcons' management was allowed to take permanent possession of the trophy because league officials decided that each time a club won three championships, that team would "retire the cup."

Meanwhile, Mulleavy's old rival, Jake Pitler, was enjoying success in the major leagues. Pitler moved up the Dodgers' chain as a manager and a coach during the war and on to Brooklyn as an interim coach in 1946. He stayed and became the Brooklyn Dodgers' first base coach in 1947,

Jackie Robinson's first year in the majors. Robinson, in 1946, was recognized as the first black in "modern times" to play organized baseball when he was signed by Branch Rickey's Dodgers and assigned to Montreal of the International League.

Robinson broke the color barrier in the 20th century, but there were many blacks in organized baseball during the 19th century. Robert Peterson, in his book *Only the Ball was White*, wrote, "in 1898 a young all-Negro team wrote the final chapter to the story of black men in white leagues during baseball's early days." And it was Jamestown that hosted this team, the Celoron Acme Colored Giants.

In 1898, three years after Honus Wagner played at Celoron Park during his rookie season, a promoter named Harry Curtis promised local fans that "we will have the strongest colored club in America." The Celoron Acme Colored Giants were poised to make history, but not as the powerhouse Curtis envisioned.

The Giants opened their season with a loss on the road in Warren, Pennsylvania on May 12, 1898. The Iron & Oil League was a primarily white league, with Jamestown's club the only all-black team. Their reception was mixed. In the case of Warren, the Giants were received with open arms and a little amusement. "The Celorons drove home from here Saturday night," wrote a Warren correspondent for *Sporting Life* magazine, "and leaving town they enlivened the air with singing—and they can sing as well as they can play. The Negroes are a jolly, gentlemanly crowd and an honor to the league."

The Giants' home opener at Celoron park was a fiasco. Curtis planned for the players of both the local club and the visiting Bradford team to be taken around Jamestown on a streetcar before the game. The Giants and their opponents were cheered on the ride from Celoron Park to the main station in Jamestown. But Curtis absent-mindedly failed to provide return tickets for the Bradford players who were given no choice but to hike back while the Giants returned by streetcar.

The cranky Bradford players spoiled the home team's opener by beating the Giants 15-4. "Celoron Bombarded, Their Fleet Sunk, and Their Forts Demolished," the *Jamestown Evening Journal* read, mimicking recent headlines describing the Spanish-American War.

Despite losing often that summer, the Giants earned respect from the Celoron Park fans for their effort. While all-black clubs elsewhere in the minor leagues had vanished, Jamestowners showed a genuine excitement at Celoron when their team showed even remote signs of life.

After a win on May 30, the *Evening Journal* read, "It was an old time enthusiastic baseball crowd and the enthusiasm of the crowd must have been communicated to the Celoron team, for they wrested victory from the Warren team after playing the best game of baseball that has been seen here this season."

But Curtis was so incompetent a general manager that he didn't even notify potential fans of game days and times. "The manager makes no effort," an angry *Evening Journal* reporter wrote, "to let the people know when a ballgame is to be expected. Many people in the city would be present had they known that a game was scheduled." The Giants' poor play certainly didn't help generate fan support. They began the season 6-17 and dropped to last place by mid-June. A game on June 17 was described in the *Evening Journal* as "one of the poorest exhibitions of ball playing ever witnessed on the Celoron grounds." By the end of June, the Giants were still in last with an 8-33 record. "The Celoron club is playing in much too fast company," the *Evening Journal* read. "The team should be strengthened or replaced by an aggregation that can make a credible showing." Attendance was miserable and the club was losing money.

On July 5, the Giants lost to Warren 12-4. Like their 1895 predecessors, a loss to Warren was the last straw for the 1898 Celoron Acme Colored Giants. "Celoron Giants Disband— A Strong Club Secured to Take Their Place," the *Evening*

Journal announced two days later. Curtis' club dispersed and none of the players from the Giants would go on to have significant careers in baseball.

While his players scattered, Curtis remained irrepressible, even lying to reporters about having had success at Celoron Park. "I have just returned from Jamestown, New York," Curtis wrote in a letter to *The Sporting News*, "where I was located with my Acme Colored Giants in the Iron & Oil League wherein we were third at the time we quit. I have a complete outfit and I am prepared to furnish a first class team, either colored or white, to play independent ball, or will go in any league." Curtis was never to be seen again in Jamestown, and apparently there were no takers for his offer to play elsewhere.

"With that team's demise," wrote David Craft is his book, *The Negro Leagues*, "a turbulent, maddening period in organized baseball had finally given way to a slightly calmer but racially segregated period in which only whites could play at the minor- and major-league levels."

A new club which had just disbanded in Louisville arrived one week after the Giants folded. When they played, they won nearly every game. But after more than two full weeks of poor weather, this club was also forced to give up the struggle at Celoron Park on August 1. "It is with a feeling of regret that I leave my friends and Jamestown, and hope some day to play here again," the well-spoken manager of this short-lived team wrote in a letter to the *Evening Journal*. "People here want a team and baseball as a pleasure and recreation if someone energetic enough would give it a little attention and money."

Five months after Mulleavy's Oilers were embarrassed in Olean, John Jachym ushered in the 1948 Falcons with caution. "I sincerely hope the fans will not expect us to win the pennant again," said Jachym during the first week in February, "because I do not think we will."

Olson was again manager and took his youthful Falcons (their average age was 18) to Hornell for their season opener against the Maple Leafs and their new manager, 1946 and 1947 Jamestown catcher, Russ Kerns. Catching and managing for Hornell, Kerns welcomed the Falcons with a three-for-three night, including a home run, to delight the big crowd and help beat the Falcons 5-3.

Olson's 1948 team was not the dominant club it was the season before, but largely due to the play of center fielder Pat Haggerty, the Falcons contended all season. Haggerty, a left-handed hitting Irishman, closely trailed Kerns for the PONY League batting title throughout the summer of 1948. By mid-August, the two matched hits in a batting race that was lost to PONY League fans amid a three-way pennant race between Jamestown, Lockport, and Hamilton. In the final 14 games of the season, Haggerty hit .567 to keep the Falcons in the race and top Kerns for the batting title with a .366 average.

Haggerty would move up in the minor leagues in 1949 and 1950 and lead his league in hitting both years. But the call to the majors never came for the Colorado-born outfielder. So Haggerty retired from baseball and began refereeing football games where his easy demeanor and athletic abilities brought him to the top of a new field; Haggerty went on to referee three Super Bowls during his long career in the National Football League.

Gerald Benjamin Kleinsmith was another member of the 1948 Falcons. From Monroe, Michigan, Kleinsmith quickly distinguished himself in the pitching rotation and got stronger as the season progressed. On August 4, the "Michigan Master" struck out 19 against Lockport to set a league record and win the game 15-1.

On the final day of August, with the pennant race deadlocked, Kleinsmith faced the Hamilton Cardinals at Municipal Stadium. There were two outs in the bottom of the ninth with the Falcons ahead 15-0 and Kleinsmith was one out away from a no-hitter. The pitch came to the plate and the ball was sliced to shallow-center. Center fielder

Haggerty had no chance to make a play, but the Falcons' shortstop charged to the outfield with his back to the base umpire. He thrust his glove out, saw the ball fall to the grass, and then gloved it on a short-hop without breaking stride. The umpire, thinking the ball was caught on a fly, raised his clenched fist and called the batter out. Judge Allen Bargar, still a city judge and a regular at Municipal Stadium, shook his head sadly. An injustice had been done.

As the fans happily filed out through the turnstiles, Judge Bargar found sports editor Frank Hyde, also the official scorer for the Falcons. "It was not a no-hitter," said Bargar. "He caught the ball on a bounce." Hyde agreed, but had no grounds for appeal. "Something ought to be done because I don't like to see that happen," insisted Bargar, "even if it does happen to the visiting team." Years later, Hyde would pass on to Bargar a copy of the PONY League record book (which Hyde had helped compile). Bargar immediately turned to the no-hit log on page nine, took out a pen from his chest pocket, and ran a streak of black ink through Kleinsmith's line. Despite Judge Bargar, the Kleinsmith no-hitter stood and became the first thrown at Municipal Stadium.

The Falcons closed out the 126-game season with three victories: 13-9 over Bradford, 13-0 over Olean, and 14-2 over Wellsville. Kleinsmith, in his first start since his "no-hitter," pitched the Olean game and struck out 20, including three in the ninth, to break his own strikeout record. Still, Olson's club fell short in their pennant drive, as Jachym said they would, and settled for second place behind Lockport.

The Falcons only needed four games to top Bradford in the best-of-five semi-finals, but Lockport proved to be their nemesis through to the end of the 1948 season. The Falcons lost the Governors Cup finals four games to one.

Less than two months after the loss to Lockport, Jachym shocked Jamestown's baseball followers with an announcement that he was selling the Falcons to the Detroit Tigers. "This has been the toughest decision I have ever had to make," Jachym told Hyde of the *Post-Journal* on October 26, 1948. "If I did not believe the move best serves my own interests I would not make it." After a co-pennant in 1946, a pennant and championship in 1947, and an appearance in the 1948 finals, Jachym's reign was over.

When Branch Rickey became general manager of the Cardinals in 1919, his organization owned one minor-league team. Twenty years later, when Jachym first met Rickey, the Cardinals owned 29 minor-league clubs. As a result of Rickey's success with the Cardinals during the Depression, other major-league teams purchased farm clubs to train their increasingly younger ballplayers in a controlled environment. As a result of the loss of local ownership, minor-league towns and cities came to be seen by major-league organizations as proving grounds for young talent rather than markets in and of themselves. By 1948, the vast majority of minor-league clubs were owned and operated by major-league front offices. In October of 1948, Jamestown became one of them.

With the coming of the farm system to the minors, it became tougher to operate independently—major-league teams had players and deep pockets. Major-league front offices were content to simply break even, or even lose a little money, in the operation of their minor-league club—losses could be written off as an investment in the future of their organizations. Independent owners like Bisgeier and Jachym, on the other hand, needed their minor-league operations to generate income.

Hyde considered the situation in his "Frankly Speaking" column. "It is not impossible that Jachym, by no means slow with an idea, saw the handwriting on the wall, realized that it would be tougher to operate as an independent owner and decided to move his franchise while it would go over the block for a good sum."

The era of financially successful independent ownership was ending and a more difficult time for the minor leagues was beginning.

Jachym was at the Falcons' spring training the following year, in 1949, on his first assignment for the Detroit Tigers as a "troubleshooter." He watched the Falcons' bus (the same one he had purchased three years earlier) drive through the gates of the Hershey, Pennsylvania ballpark where the Falcons held spring training since Jachym took over as owner. Jachym stood at the door waiting for the 1949 Falcons to step down one by one, led by their manager, Marv Olson. "This is the first time I really regret having sold the Jamestown franchise." Jachym said to Hyde who was, as always, covering spring training for the *Post-Journal.* "All this spring training activity and preparing for another pennant contender makes me a little homesick, if you know what I mean." Jachym stepped aside and let the club pass.

Two years later, after promoting a failed barnstorming tour with former tennis star and legendary male chauvinist Bobby Riggs, the 31-year-old Jachym would march into the office of 81-year-old Washington Senators' president Clark W. Griffith. Jachym had just purchased a large block of the club's stocks and came to inform Griffith that they were business partners. Jachym would never be a welcome addition to the Senators' organization because Griffith resented the younger businessman as a major partner. Six months after the purchase, Jachym sold his shares and moved out of baseball entirely. The former Falcons' owner, who borrowed money from his parents to buy the team after World War II, would become a multimillionaire in a variety of business ventures and remain an influential businessman for decades.

F I V E

THE OPENING WEEKS OF THE 1949 SEASON BROUGHT high expectations. Jamestowners packed Municipal Stadium, each ticket they purchased further assuring Detroit management that they had made a shrewd move in purchasing the Falcons. The new PONY league president, Vince McNamara, was beginning a stay in office that would last 37 years. On the field, the Falcons were expected to do well. "To death and taxes you can add another sure thing," Hyde wrote, "and that is that the 1949 Jamestown Falcons are the best looking early season contenders since Greg Mulleavy's bone crushers of 1941 and 1942."

Olson returned as Falcons' manager, heading a Detroit farm team that was younger, faster, and stronger than the PONY League teams of the early 1940s. The Falcons were "prospects," investments under the close watch of Detroit as they traveled through Pennsylvania, Ontario, and New York. The Tigers gave Jamestown, according to Olson, a "bunch of fence-busters."

Willie "Fireball" Furlong, raised in the neighboring town of Salamanca, was one of the Falcons' pitchers in 1949. During a nine-game win streak, Furlong won two ballgames, giving up a combined seven hits. After the second win, Hyde wrote that Furlong could probably become mayor of Salamanca. Furlong was on his way to becoming the 1949 PONY League pitching champion with a 16-5 record and 1.89 ERA. The local boy was honored that summer with a "Bill Furlong Night" and presented a suitcase as a gift.

Before the last scheduled night of the season, Olson's Falcons were tied with the Bradford Phillies for first place. As the schedule would have it, the two teams were to meet for a doubleheader in Bradford. The Phillies took the first game easily. The best the Falcons could hope for was a win in the second game, ending the regular season tied up, which would force a one-game playoff. The second game was 4-4 in the bottom of the ninth inning with a Bradford runner on second. The Phillies' fans, and the few hundred Jamestowners who made the trip to Bradford, blew into their cupped hands to keep warm.

Danny Carnevale, Bradford's cool skipper and 1949 league batting champion and RBI leader, stood on second base, clapping his hands for his teammate at the plate. A line drive to left field sent Carnevale sprinting around third, all eyes on his tall, dark frame. There was no throw home as he hopped onto home plate. Falcons fans, having grown accustomed to winning big games, watched in disbelief.

The Falcons finished in second place and played third-place Hamilton in the semi-finals. But after Carnevale scored, many baseball fans lost interest in the post-season. With the Falcons down three games to one, Olson changed into his Falcons home uniform—a white "J" on the center of his hat, "Falcons" stitched in script lettering across the chest of the jersey, baggy pants with stirrups—for the final time. "Fireball" Furlong threw a four-hitter against the Cardinals, a team he dominated all season, but Olson's "fence-busters" could manage just one run. With less than a thousand fans on hand, the Falcons bowed from the playoffs.

Sports editor Frank Hyde had watched from the press box throughout the series, seeing empty seats and sulking faces. Men in dark suits and hats, and women in long coats covering cotton dresses, had once filled the park, rooting and hollering for Bisgeier's and Jachym's Falcons.

"Jamestown fans are a pretty spoiled lot," wrote Hyde the day after Furlong's four-hit loss. "They are flush with victory after victory, well fed with pennants and playoff trophies. Their sense of values has been dulled with an overdose of 'victory serum,' and a year that fails to produce a flag winner is a 'lost season.'"

Eight months later, Ray Caldwell (struck by lightning on the pitcher's mound in 1919) walked through the art deco lobby of the Hotel Jamestown with another former major-league pitcher from Jamestown, Erik "Swat" Erickson. The two were there for a "Meet the Manager" reception—an official welcome for the new Falcons' manager, Bob Shawkey, which took place just prior to the opening of the 1950 season. Erickson, Caldwell, and Shawkey all played in the major leagues during the early 1920s.

Caldwell was Shawkey's teammate on the Yankees from 1916 to 1918 before being traded to the Indians. Erickson's Washington Senators of the early 1920s routinely fell to Shawkey's Yankees. In 1924, the Senators finally grabbed the pennant from their American League rivals and went on to beat John McGraw's Giants in the World Series, but Erickson (57-34 lifetime record during seven years in the majors) had been sent down to the minors. He watched the Series from the stands in Washington. "See, when they got rid of me they won," Erickson commented.

Erickson was born in Göteborg, Sweden in 1895 and, soon after, moved with his family to Western Pennsylvania, then on to Jamestown in 1912. They joined a growing community in Jamestown which had formed a loosely defined "Swede Hill" on the east side of town. Swat's older brother, Harry, was mayor of Jamestown and would toss the ceremonial first pitch at Celoron Park to open the 1939 PONY League season. (Mayor Harry Erickson was also the man who formed the Citizen's Stadium Committee in 1940 that placed Ernest Kessler and Judge Allan Bargar in charge of building what would become Municipal Stadium.) Swat's son, Burwin Erickson, would be a Falcons' pitcher under Mulleavy in 1941 and with Olson in 1946.

In the summer of 1912, Erickson was a lanky 17-year-old with a blazing fastball. He was playing for LeRow's Semi-Pros at Celoron Park when a scout from the Texas League came to see the teenager pitch. "Think you could throw like that down at Dallas?" he asked. "I could try," Erickson said. Erickson pitched in Dallas in 1913 and made it to the majors in 1914 with John McGraw's New York Giants.

The last time McGraw dealt with a Jamestown pitcher was when Hugh Bedient's Red Sox beat his Giants in the 1912 World Series. (In 1913, McGraw lost to future Falcons' manager Bob Shawkey and the Philadelphia A's.) Late in the 1914 season, the fiery McGraw and his club were struggling to catch the Boston Braves who held a narrow lead over the Giants when Erickson made his major-league debut against the Phillies in Philadelphia. With the game tied in the late innings, Erickson cut off a throw from the outfield with the go-ahead runner rounding third. He faked a throw home but the delay allowed the runner to dive back to third base. The runner later scored from third and the Giants lost.

"Son, never bluff in this game!" McGraw yelled at Erickson. "Throw that ball!" Erickson recalled years later that "McGraw was a rough cuss, but he was fair and firm and his players respected him." That was the only game Erickson pitched in 1914 for the Giants before being sent back down to the minors.

The following spring, Erickson fractured the index finger of his pitching hand on a line drive. He was sent to an "expert" in Waco, Texas who broke and unsuccessfully reset the bone. The finger caused Erickson excruciating pain, but he returned to the mound quickly and was assigned to the Hustlers of Rochester, New York. He could do no better than a .500 record when a fan stopped him after a home game. "Want to cure that finger?" the fan asked Erickson. The Red Wing fan didn't wait for a reply. "Just cut a hole through a lemon and slide it over the finger. Leave it on all night." Erickson was ready to try anything to save his flagging career. He followed the prescription and, when he removed the shriveled fruit the next morning, the pain was gone. "You won't believe it," Erickson later said, "but it never bothered me again."

His finger healed just in time for the Rochester club because they had recently lost several pitchers to injuries. Erickson, now healthy, pitched almost every other game. The Swede won 20 games in 40 days at one stretch in 1915, prompting future International League President Clark Shaughnessy to describe Erickson's recovery as a "miracle of baseball." During the off-season, the Detroit Tigers picked up Erickson. He pitched in the majors for the Tigers and then the Senators, for the next six seasons.

Thirty-five years after his "miracle" season still a Jamestown resident, Erickson walked through the Hotel Jamestown with Caldwell. A few of the 1950 Falcons stood to one side, clean-cut and dressed in blue or gray suits like their older hosts. Through the crowd, Erickson and Caldwell caught a glimpse of Shawkey, their one-time American League pitching rival. The aging men converged, shook hands, and exchanged pleasantries.

Shawkey, 60 years old in 1950, had thrown the first official pitch at Yankee Stadium in 1923, won 20 games four times with the Yankees, and appeared in five World Series during the 1920s. Shawkey also managed the Yankees in 1930 to a third-place finish.

Frank Hyde's *Post-Journal* staff photographer caught the

threesome's attention and asked them to turn to the camera. Erickson crossed his hands above his waist and Caldwell gave a slight sneer. Shawkey gave a far-off half-smile, perhaps wondering how a man who often shared the field with Babe Ruth had become a 60-year-old manager for a Class D club.

Much of the 1950 season would be recorded by Jerry Lawson, the Falcons' radio voice for station WJOC-Jamestown. Lawson grew up rooting for the Falcons of the early 1940s. As an adolescent, he wanted more than anything to be bat boy for Greg Mulleavy's great clubs. He never did get the chance to carry John Newman's or John Pollock's bat. Instead, he followed the Falcons from the bleachers with the rest of Jamestown's faithful.

Like many of the ballplayers—and their owner, Harry Bisgeier—Lawson was called overseas during World War II. After the war, Bisgeier returned to the front office and Lawson took a job with WJOC, the local radio station which carried only a handful of Falcons games in 1946. In 1949, WJOC began carrying every game and Lawson was chosen to be their play-by-play man.

On opening night in 1950, Lawson and Hyde watched from the press box as the mayor addressed the crowd. Only a few words had left his mouth when a screech of feedback blared from the park's speakers. "That was enough anyway, Mayor!" a fan yelped.

Hyde noted the episode in his narrow reporters' pad. On the field, a *Post-Journal* staff photographer snapped pictures. Lawson prepared to begin his broadcast. None of the three could have imagined that this awkward start was an appropriate beginning to a decade that would end in disaster for Jamestown's minor-league baseball organization.

The season began poorly for the Falcons. They lost on opening night and kept on losing. Their stone-faced manager came into PONY League parks without a smile and left with few words. There was a bright spot that summer, however, and Lawson helped capture it.

Lawson did not make the road trips with Hyde. Instead, a Western Union employee took his spot in the press box and tapped the game to Lawson, who sat at the WJOC studio in Jamestown. When the Falcons brought their last-place record into Lockport on July 20, Lawson followed from the studio via short telegraph messages which streamed in on a thin strip of paper like a stock ticker.

Dick Fortune, a small southpaw who would only win four games in 1950, was the starter that night. In Lockport, Fortune peered into the catcher's waiting mitt and threw a curveball which fell in for a strike. The Western Union telegraph operator tapped a message to Lawson. A strip of paper which read "S1C" stuttered into Lawson's hand. Lawson spoke into his microphone: "He winds. A curveball over the plate for strike one." Another message appeared: "B1OS." "Ball one, outside," Lawson said. "The count evens at one and one." A little more than two hours later, Fortune threw his final pitch of the night to complete a no-hitter. It was only the third by a Falcons' pitcher and the fourth in PONY League history.

Despite Fortune's performance, the Falcons were still losing. Shawkey tried different lineups and Detroit sent new players to Jamestown, including pitcher Frank Lary. A freckle-faced, 20-year-old from Alabama, Lary would be known as "The Yankee Killer" in the majors for his dominance of the New York club (28-13 lifetime against the Yankees and under .500 against the rest of the league during his 12 years in the majors). Lary would spend most of his career with the Tigers, winning 21 games in 1956 and 23 in 1961.

Lary was signed in 1950 by a Detroit scout named Howard Camp. Camp was driving through Alabama to see another player when his fan belt broke and he was forced to stop at a garage. While the mechanic was fixing the car he asked Camp what he was doing in Alabama. Camp told him he was a scout and who he was going to see. "You're wasting your time," the mechanic said. "Stay right here and see Frank Lary. He's the best thing in the area." Camp stayed the night, saw Lary throw, and signed the young pitcher on the spot.

Lary joined the Falcons on July 25. Five days later, Shawkey gave Lary three innings of relief work against Hamilton and started him at Olean three days after that. Lary pitched the entire game and the Falcons won his first start 8-1. He won five and lost two in his 10 appearances in 1951 and impressed Shawkey, the former Yankees' pitcher. "He is a strong, cool kid who doesn't get shaken up out there," said the Falcons manager. "He'll make a money pitcher some day, a real clutch man."

Even with Lary, the news never got better during the summer of 1950. Lawson, Hyde, and the *Post-Journal* staff photographer all told the same story. The 1950 Falcons finished in sixth place after six seasons of finishing either first or second in the PONY League. Shawkey cleared his belongings out of his tiny Municipal Stadium office and characteristically left without a word.

During the fall of 1950, the infield grass of Municipal Stadium turned its annual brown and, by early winter, was covered with snow. A car door slammed. Moments later, two sets of feet left their imprints in the fresh, white blanket. Falcons' general manager Cedric Tallis, who would later work for the Yankees and the Kansas City Royals, was leading the new field manager into the ballpark.

Tony Lupien, like the more weathered Shawkey whom he replaced, had a stay in the majors. He graduated from Harvard in 1936 and rose through the major-league ranks during the late 1930s and early 1940s. Lupien played for the Red Sox and then the Phillies until he was drafted in 1945. One year later, the first baseman returned to the United States and was immediately traded to a minor-league club.

Lupien filed a protest with Major League Baseball Commissioner Happy Chandler, claiming that the trade violated the National Defense Act which protected the jobs of military veterans. Chandler took the side of the owners, turning down Lupien's protest. Lupien played in the minors for two years, then in 1948, returned to the majors for one season with the Chicago White Sox.

Through the fog of his breath, the dark-eyed, French-Canadian Lupien watched and listened as Tallis scraped off home plate. "I want you to do something with me," Tallis said. "We are going to stand back-to-back here at home plate. You look out into center field and I'm going to look up in the grandstand." Lupien, who in addition to his managing duties would play first base for the Falcons in 1952, followed instructions. "This is the way we are going to operate," Tallis' voice came from over Lupien's shoulder. "Everything I'm looking at is in my domain and everything you're looking at is in your domain."

When the snow melted and the 1951 season began, Lupien moved into Judge Bargar's house, his home for the summer, and ruled his "domain" with a breezy demeanor and a hot bat. Through much of the season, Lupien led the league in hitting. He would finish among the league's best with a .368 average.

Lupien was also blessed with a strong supporting cast which included four more .300-plus hitters. One was Frank Bolling, a slick-fielding second baseman from Mobile, Alabama. Bolling would spend 12 years in the majors, including All-Star years with the Milwaukee Braves in 1961 and 1962.

Another was a tough New Jersey kid named Emil Karlik, who Lupien first saw play in spring training a few months earlier. The Falcons needed a right fielder and Lupien had to decide between a $10,000 "bonus baby" and Karlik, who was signed for $175 a month. Lupien chose Karlik. "He had the guts of a cat burglar," The Falcon's manager said. "He could steal a hot stove right out of the kitchen and I just fell in love with the way this kid played baseball."

Lupien and his fearless right fielder engaged the Olean Oilers, Jamestown's perennial rivals, in a season-long dog-fight for the top spot in the PONY League. Lupien charmed Jamestowners with his genuine fondness for the city and its people. His easy-going demeanor was a refreshing change from Shawkey's stoicism the previous year. The engaging manager became so linked to the team that Frank Hyde began calling the Falcons the "Lupienmen."

On September 3, the final day of the regular season, the Falcons were one game behind the Olean Oilers. Lupien's Falcons would have to beat the visiting Bradford Phillies and hope for an Olean loss to Wellsville. The bottom of the eighth was about to begin with Bradford up 4-3 when an announcement came over the loudspeaker: "In the bottom of the eighth in Olean, the Wellsville Rockets lead the Olean Oilers 5-2." The crowd cheered. A win by the Falcons would place them into a tie with the Oilers for the pennant.

The Falcon's lead-off man popped out. A walk put the next batter on first. The third man up ripped a line drive up the middle which was deflected by the pitcher and fell to the grass for an infield single. The Lupienmen had the tying and go-ahead runners on first and second, prompting Bradford's manager to make a pitching change.

Karlik, who led the league in doubles and triples, waited in the on-deck circle. When the left-handed reliever was finished with his warm-up tosses, Karlik stepped up to the left side of the plate. Karlik ran the count to two balls and two strikes. Calmly, he called time and met Lupien for a conference halfway down the third base line.

"Skip, this guy's pitching me outside," Karlik said. "I can hit him. Get them running, I'm going to poke one into left field."

Lupien raised his eyebrows and breathed deeply. "Sure you can get a chunk of the ball?"

"Right, skip," Karlik said. "You get them running."

Lupien turned and walked back to the third base coaching box. He clapped to get the attention of his runners and flashed the hit-and-run sign. The Phillies' lefty went into his windup and the runner took off. Mouths shot open in the stands as the pitch came to the plate. Karlik reached for the outside fastball and drove the ball to left field. Lupien jerked his head over his shoulder as Karlik's drive flew over the third base bag. The runner representing the tying run sprinted home while the ball rolled all the way to the left field fence. Lupien waved the winning run home and Karlik trotted into third.

Bradford's pitcher retired the next two Falcons to end the eighth inning, then the Phillies failed to score in the top of the ninth. The Lupienmen won by a score of 5-4. The Oilers failed to come back in Olean, so the Falcons again found themselves tied for first place at the end of a regular schedule.

The next night, at a packed Bradner Stadium in Olean, the Falcons lost to the Oilers in a one-game playoff and finished the 1951 season in second place. As a result, Lupien's club played the third-place Hornell Dodgers in the semi-finals. Managed by former Falcons' batting champ Doc Alexson, the Dodgers took four out of five games to end Jamestown's baseball season. The Dodgers, with help from their pitcher Henry Franklin (the PONY's first black player) went on to defeat Olean in the finals.

The Falcons had already parted ways after the loss to Hornell, but the season wasn't over for other baseball men familiar to Frank Hyde's readers in Jamestown. Nellie Fox, the former 16-year-old Falcons' center fielder, was in his second season at second base in Chicago and on his way to becoming a fan favorite and Hall of Famer with the White Sox. "Jumping" Jake Pitler, the former Olean villain, had moved all the way up the Dodgers' chain to Brooklyn; in September of 1951, Pitler was still first base coach at Ebbets Field. Up the East River from Brooklyn, at the Polo Grounds in northern Manhattan, Sal Maglie was in the World Series. Maglie started and lost game four for the Giants and his club went on to lose the Series in six games.

In May of 1952, eight months after Karlik's game-winning hit, Tony Lupien sat back in his seat on the Falcons' bus with a brand new team. He listened to the bus driver, Jerry Klein, serenade an underachieving Falcon's pitcher. The short, round driver sang through and around the butt of an almost finished cigar:

> *If you threw a curveball that broke like a bomb,*
> *You must have left it in the league you came from.*
> *$85,000 our scouts paid for you, but you keep on losing*
> *twelve-fifty to two.*
> *Why don't you quit baseball?*
> *Try something else instead.*
> *If you'd win a ballgame, the team would drop dead.*
> *If you're a great pitcher, it's now plain to see,*
> *You've kept it a secret from me.*

During the mid-1920s, Klein had been the driver and chaperone for teenage Jamestowner Lucille Ball. In 1952, he served almost the same function for the Falcons. Klein was the team's trainer, bus driver, and all-around caretaker. At times, he even sold ice pops in the stands. His most important role, however, was to keep the young ballplayers loose.

One of those young men was shortstop Mike Illitch, an unassuming 18-year-old from Michigan signed to a $3,000 contract by the Tigers to fill out Jamestown's roster. His time with the 1952 Falcons was short; he was promoted to Detroit's Class C club on June 20. In 1954, a knee injury would force Illitch to quit baseball. His playing days behind him, Illitch opened a pizza parlor in Garden City, Michigan. He called it Little Caesar's and it spawned the wildly successful restaurant chain. In 1990, Illitch purchased the Detroit Tigers—the organization that had signed him almost 40 years earlier. In 1994, Illitch's Tigers would revive their long-dormant affiliation with Jamestown, placing him at the head of baseball operations at the ballpark where he began his career.

Thanks to another heavy-hitting year from Lupien, and the steady bat of their young catcher Charlie Lau, the Falcons were on their way to a second-place PONY League finish. No one was happier about the team's success than Flo White and her mother, two of the Falcons' biggest fans.

Flo, as her friends called her, was an attractive 19-year-old brunette in 1951 and went to every Falcons game during Lupien's first season. During the spring before the 1951 season began, Flo had won two season tickets at a dinner raffle. She gave the other to her mother. Seats 10 and 11 in row B on the first base side of the grandstand became their second home. At the ballpark in 1952, Flo and her mother screamed for Lupien, Lau, and Illitch. One evening, two farmers—brothers from a neighboring village—gave Flo a small but loud goat bell. They suggested that it might help preserve her voice.

Flo's mother, born in England, took to baseball immediately because, she said, the sport reminded her of cricket. They both took to the players. By mid-season of 1952, their second season as regulars, it was not uncommon for Flo's mother to invite Lau and his teammates to her home for a hot meal. Flo never knew who would be at the dinner table when she came home from work.

On the streets of Jamestown, Flo's mother would often be given rides. "Hey, Mom! Where you goin'?" a carload of ballplayers would scream to Flo's mother. "Hop in!" they'd insist.

Thirty-eight years later, Flo would sit in the third-base bleachers of Jamestown's ballpark under cloudy skies. By 1990, the park's name had changed once and the team's name had changed several times. Flo had become a white-haired mother of three and moved from the grandstand to the bleachers. Her mother had passed away years before.

She still had season tickets and the goat bell on her lap though. As she glanced at the visiting club's roster, she looked in shock at the name "Charlie Lau." She thought it was a cruel joke. Lau was listed as hitting instructor of the Utica Blue Sox, which she knew was impossible. Flo had followed his career through the newspaper and knew that the Charlie Lau who ate at her mother's table had died of cancer in 1984.

By the early 1980s, Charlie Lau had become the most influential hitting instructor in baseball. His playing days ended in the late 1960s but his book, *The Art of Hitting .300*, became the bible to his approach. George Brett and Reggie Jackson dramatically improved their hitting under the guidance of Lau. The White Sox honored their deceased coach by wearing arm bands on their uniforms the season after he died.

Flo asked the players about the "Lau" on the roster and soon discovered that the hitting instructor was Charlie Lau Jr., Charlie Lau's son. Flo introduced herself to the young man.

"You must have known my father," Lau Jr. said.

"I sure did," Flo answered.

They chatted briefly, but the game at hand called them both to their posts—Lau Jr. to the dugout and Flo to the bleachers. The clouds broke during the fourth inning and the game was delayed. Most fans fled, but Flo and a handful more sought shelter in the grandstand.

Lau Jr. joined her and asked Flo to tell him about his father. He had no idea that Jamestown's field had been the one upon which his father began his career. In fact, he knew very little of his father, who died when Lau Jr. was only 19. Flo talked throughout the long delay, telling him her memories of Charlie Lau as a rookie catcher and a young man away from home.

In mid-June of 1952, Doc Alexson came to Jamestown with his Hornell Dodgers and Flo looked out at the field to see Charlie Lau behind the plate and Tony Lupien at first base. Hornell's rookie shortstop, Maury Wills, remembered the game years later. "Al Campanis came to watch us play when we were in Jamestown. I know I wanted to do well and did." Wills had two hits and Alexson singled home the winning run for the Dodgers in the 10th inning to beat the Falcons. "So I went out that night to celebrate and stayed out a little bit later than I was supposed to." When Wills returned to the hotel, Campanis caught him past curfew. "I never did turn that report to the Dodgers that said you stayed out late," Campanis told Wills later in both of their careers. It was the right move—Wills would be a five time All-Star with the Los Angeles Dodgers and steal 104 bases in 1962.

Despite the loss to Hornell, the Falcons finished the 1952 season in second place, two games behind Hamilton. Lupien's club strolled through the playoffs with four straight over Olean in the semi-finals and another four straight over Alexson's Hornell Dodgers in the finals (the eight straight post-season victories was an unprecedented feat in PONY League history). The fourth game of the finals, a Falcons' victory in Hornell, was won with a big inning in front of 1,234 Hornell fans. After a walk and a double, Lupien walked to load the bases. A Maury Wills' error allowed two runs to score, then Lau was hit by a pitch. A double by the Falcons' third baseman, Bob Neebling, drove in two more runs. The Falcons went on to win the game 5-4 and the Governors Cup shifted from Alexson's Dodgers, who had won it all in 1951, to Lupien's Falcons. Despite their fourth league championship, Falcons' attendance at Municipal Stadium dropped from 73,099 in 1951 to 56,408 in 1952. League attendance was also down (by 17 percent) from the previous year.

Lupien left at the end of the 1952 playoff sweep and was replaced by Danny Carnevale. Falcons fans remembered Carnevale best as the Bradford manager and PONY batting champion whose Phillies swept a doubleheader on the final day of the 1949 season to edge Jamestown out of a pennant. Carnevale was the tall, dark figure who represented the winning run in the second game. "It is one of those things that come once in a player's lifetime and I still get a thrill when I think of being able to participate in it," said Carnevale. "We went down to the last day—down to two men out in the ninth inning of the last game of the season—to win the pennant!" Carnevale was a winner. The clubs he managed in and out of the PONY League won pennants four times between 1948 and 1952.

Soft-spoken and amiable, Carnevale watched from the home dugout in Jamestown as his Falcons went out and crushed their opponents. Hornell, Olean, Bradford. . . it didn't matter to Carnevale's wrecking crew. PONY League clubs walked unwittingly onto the field, in clean gray uniforms, their caps straight and snug, and two or three hours later scrambled back to their bus, lucky to escape with the rags on their backs. Carnevale's Falcons finished with a record of 88 wins and 37 losses, 18 games better than their closest competition. The 1953 Falcons were the most dominant team the PONY League had ever seen, and would stay that way for 21 years.

One of the reasons for their success was pitcher Bob Shaw, a 20-year-old Bronx boy who would spend 11 years in the majors, including two World Series starts in 1959 for the White Sox. Shaw won 108 games in his major-league career and was known as an eccentric off the field. In 1952, he was signed by legendary scout Cy Williams who also had to bail Shaw out of jail later that year for chopping down Christmas trees on private property.

In the summer of 1953, Shaw was involved in another mishap. "We were in our hotel room playing Pinochle," remembered Al Taylor, a pitcher for the Falcons who would be a long-time Jamestown-area resident. "A few guys had to go to the bathroom. [The hotel] had outdoor bathrooms so we took a break at about midnight. This left-hander, Bob Ward, comes back with a big fire extinguisher. We asked him, 'What are you going to do with this?' He says, 'I'm going to see how it works.'"

"So Shaw told him, 'Just turn it upside down. That's how it works.' Well Ward started it and the thing wouldn't stop. So he stuck it out the window. We were on the fourth floor of this horseshoe-type motel. The thing is spraying all over the place, onto other rooms and all over the wires.

"'What are we going to do?' Shaw asked. 'Why don't we set the room on fire?'"

"I said, 'You're going to set the whole motel on fire!' So a few guys broke into the maid's room and took some mops to clean up, but they couldn't do too much. When we got on the bus in the morning, everyone looked straight ahead. Then Carnevale started hollering. 'Who was in room 405?' Nobody answered. 'Who was in room 405?!' Ward answered that it was him. He got shipped out the next day. Right out of Jamestown."

Shaw stayed, however, and won 10 games for the 1953 Falcons. Forty years later, in 1993, Carnevale was in Jupiter, Florida. He stopped at the local mall and looked up at the entrance sign. It read, "The Bob Shaw Plaza." Shaw had become a millionaire in real estate.

The 1953 season also saw the first annual "Jamestown Sports Hall of Fame Night." During the seventh inning stretch of a home game, two sports figures—one "modern-day" and one "veteran"—were honored. Radio announcer Jerry Lawson served as master of ceremonies from the pitcher's mound and introduced the guests, who stood behind him on the infield. Between second and third base were "veteran award" nominees Ray Caldwell, Hugh Bedient, and Erik Erickson. Beside the three retired ballplayers stood PONY League President Vince McNamara, Frank Hyde, and the mayor of Jamestown.

Chosen by a ballot of Jamestowners as the first veteran to be given the honor, Erickson stepped forward to receive a framed certificate representing the permanent plaque that was to be installed at the Jamestown Sports Hall of Fame. (Caldwell would receive the honor the following year and Bedient the year after that.) Hyde then announced the name of the modern-day winner, All-Star New York Yankees outfielder, Irv Noren.

Noren's family owned the town's famed Swedish "Noren Bakery." When he was 12 years old, his family moved to Pasadena (Ca.), but Noren's bakery remained under new owners. Noren began his professional career in Branch

Rickey's mushrooming, post-war Dodgers farm system. Noren's abilities went largely unrecognized with the Dodgers and he was traded by Rickey to the Senators. The Washington organization, soon to be part-owned by John Jachym, assigned him to the Hollywood Stars of the Pacific Coast League in 1949. With the Stars, Noren caught the attention of owner Clark Griffith, who signed him for $50,000, one of the largest major-league contracts of that time. Noren hit .295 as a rookie with the Senators and would continue to produce in the majors for another 11 years. In 1952, he was traded to the Yankees, who won the World Series in 1952 and 1953. When his name was announced at the "Jamestown Sports Hall of Fame Night" in 1953, Noren was with the Yankees in the Bronx but expressed regret that he could not be present at Municipal Stadium in a note to the fans.

There was no pennant race that summer for the Falcons because Carnevale's Jamestown club won the league by 18 games, a feat matched only by Olson's 1947 Falcons. Shaw and the rest of the pennant-winning Falcons cruised through the playoffs, winning eight of nine games and falling just one game short of repeating the 1952 club's playoff sweep.

After a semi-finals sweep, the finals began tied at one game apiece. The Falcons and the Cardinals made the hour-and-a-half trip to Hamilton, Canada for games three, four, and five. Flo and her mother also made the drive north, despite the windy 48-degree night. The Falcons blanked Hamilton 3-0 to take a two-games-to-one lead, but when the players returned to the bus Jerry Klein told them that their belongings had been stolen.

When Flo White and her mother woke up the next morning in Jamestown, they heard on the radio that the Falcons' bus had been robbed. They listened in dismay as the newscaster went on to report that when Klein returned to the bus at the end of the game the small rear window of the bus had been smashed and over $3,000 in valuables and cash had been stolen. The report added that the team's hotel stay for the remaining two nights was already paid in full, but all remaining meal money had been looted.

Flo and her mother jumped into their car and drove back to Hamilton. When they arrived at the small roadside motel where the club was staying they saw the players milling around outside, hungry and without recourse. The two women fed a large group of the Falcons at a nearby diner. With their bellies full, and the White's in the stands, the Falcons beat the Cardinals that night, and again the next night, to capture Jamestown's fifth Governors Cup.

The season complete, Flo and her mother offered to drive Bob Shaw and two other Falcons back to Jamestown. When they arrived back in the dark Municipal Stadium parking lot, Bob Shaw—whose keys had been stolen from the bus—crawled under his car to retrieve a spare that he'd hidden, while Flo, her mother, and the remaining two Falcons stayed in the White's car. While Shaw was searching for the key, bright police spotlights came on, "catching" the Falcons' pitcher. A policeman called for Shaw and the group in the White's car to identify themselves. They did and the police explained that they had been watching the cars around the clock in case the robbers from Hamilton made an attempt to steal any cars from the lot.

S I X

THE BLEEDING HAD TO STOP. THE DETROIT TIGERS' front office needed to break even, or at least come close to breaking even, with their Jamestown operation in 1954. Since purchasing the Falcons from John Jachym in 1949, the Tigers lost more than double what they paid. Detroit officials decided that the slide could not continue.

Detroit's Jamestown Falcons weren't losing money because of poor teams. Since the Tigers purchased the team, the Falcons went to the playoffs every year except Shawkey's ill-fated 1950 season and won two Governors Cups. In two consecutive finals appearances, in 1953 and 1954, the Falcons wiped out their opponents in a total of eight out of nine games.

In 1949, the first season the Tigers owned the Falcons, attendance at Municipal Stadium topped 110,000. By 1953, attendance barely topped 49,000. The PONY League attendance took a similar nose-dive, from over 600,000 in

1949 to 291,000 in 1953. The crowds wouldn't be the same in Jamestown—or the minors as a whole—for a long time.

Still, not all clubs were sliding. The general managers who drew the highest attendance were those who understood that you could no longer fling open the stadium gates and wait for a stampede of fans. Running a ballclub in the 1950s required salesmanship.

In the spring of 1954, a man named Hillman Lyons was hired by Detroit to be the Falcons' general manager and given the job of bringing fans back to baseball in Jamestown. Before coming to Jamestown, Lyons became general manager in Paris, Illinois in 1952. The year before he arrived, Paris drew 14,300 fans. In 1952, his club drew 75,998. In 1953, Lyons cast a similar spell over Danville, Kentucky (population 10,000), where he drew an unprecedented 66,000 fans and was named *The Sporting News* Lower Minor League Executive of the Year.

Lyons graduated from Vanderbilt University in the spring of 1939 and caught for several minor-league clubs before joining the Marines in 1944. During the war, Lyons received bayonet wounds in both legs and a bullet in his spine. His wounds healed during a nine-month convalescence but, despite a brief comeback attempt, his playing days were over.

Jamestown was a new town for Lyons, but not for some former Falcons who stayed after their PONY League days were over, like Johnny Newman and Greg Mulleavy. Mulleavy's son, Greg Jr., would never forget the sight of Newman driving a city bus. Children, he later recalled, would hop on Newman's bus just to sit and talk, even if they didn't want to go where the bus happened to be taking them. They'd watch and listen to the driver who had become so obese that the wide steering wheel made a groove in his belly as he drove.

During the 1954 off-season, Mulleavy was still assistant manager of the men's department at Bigelow's, where he had worked for over a decade. When spring arrived, Mulleavy returned to his job as scout with the Brooklyn Dodgers, the organization he had been with since 1946 when Jachym referred him to Branch Rickey.

Shortstop John O'Neil, who played for Mulleavy in 1941, was back with the Falcons for the 1954 season. His nickname was "Scooter"—a name Jamestown fans later gave to Clem Koshorek, 5-foot 2-inch shortstop of the 1946 Falcons. O'Neil, like Koshorek, met his wife in Jamestown and, though he moved up in organized baseball to the majors with the Philadelphia Phillies for 46 games in 1946, he remained tied to the town. "I have a heckuva lot of pleasant memories about my days in Jamestown," he said in 1949 as a shortstop for the Hollywood Stars, then a Washington Senators farm club. With the Stars in 1949, O'Neil shared the spotlight with Jamestown-born Irv Noren, soon to be a major-leaguer and member of the Jamestown Sports Hall of Fame.

"Scooter" O'Neil stayed with the Stars of the Pacific Coast League until 1953, when his starting shortstop job was taken away by, of all people, Clem "Scooter" Koshorek. After attaining the fifth highest average on the Pirates in 1952, Koshorek was sent down to Hollywood, by then a Pittsburgh farm team. O'Neil was signed by the Tigers to play one last season—his 14th in professional baseball. He was assigned to the Falcons and returned to Jamestown for the 1954 Falcons season and to establish a permanent home there.

O'Neil would hit .298 in 26 games for the 1954 Falcons though the team played sloppy baseball and threatened to nose-dive into last place by early June. During a three-game stretch, four Falcons were caught off base and three were thrown out at the plate. Falcons' manager Danny Litwhiler, an outfielder who played in the majors for 11 years, including a World Series against the St. Louis Cardinals in 1944, was under growing pressure to get his club to play better baseball. In mid-June of 1954, the 38-year-old Litwhiler got hurt and took himself out of the lineup. When he returned, the Falcons won four of five games but Detroit officials had already decided that Jamestown's club wasn't playing to their potential and fired Litwhiler.

"The ax fell on Dan Litwhiler with the cold and sudden savagery that is so much a part of baseball, leaving the thinning ranks of PONY League followers here gasping for breath," wrote sports editor Frank Hyde. "The Falcons were not winning. Detroit wanted the Falcons to win. So the answer is simple: fire the manager." Litwhiler was replaced with Wayne Blackburn, a stocky Scotch-Irishman with a crewcut and boundless energy. In organized baseball as a player, manager, and then a scout since 1936, Blackburn was expected to breathe life into the Falcons.

The Falcons immediately began playing better baseball and winning ballgames. Jamestown's club climbed out of seventh place and soon into fifth. Their pitching staff, led by 16-5 PONY League Rookie of the Year Tom Van Remmen and 16-6 PONY League pitching champ Bob Mische, helped move the team all the way up to second place with one game remaining.

On the final evening of the season, the Falcons won their game in Bradford to jump into first place over Corning. A raucous, albeit premature, locker room celebration followed. Two hours later, Corning won their game and took back first place and the pennant from Jamestown.

The Falcons of 1954 knocked Wellsville out of the semi-finals in three straight games to qualify for the Governors Cup finals again. After winning in 1952 and 1953, the Falcons of 1954 were only a series away from "retiring the cup" again. But Corning, the team which, just two weeks before, had edged them out for the pennant, beat the Falcons in five games to win the league championship.

More important than a league championship, however, was the attendance at Municipal Stadium. Lyons, a gifted marketer, almost doubled the attendance figures of the previous season—49,023 in 1953 to 86,460 in 1954. In October, only one month after the finals loss to Corning, Lyons was lured away from Jamestown and named general manager of the Buffalo Bisons by Detroit Tigers' management, still owners of both the Falcons and the Bisons. (Dan Carnevale, manager for the Falcons two seasons earlier, was named field manager of the Bisons.) Eighteen applications came to Detroit executives from men who felt they could fill Lyons' shoes as general manager of the Falcons. Jerry Lawson, better known as the radio voice of the Falcons, was chosen for the job.

Lawson took over the Falcons with enthusiasm. He trudged through the snow to meet with local businessmen he knew as friends and acquaintances since childhood. He drove to neighboring towns to attract new season-ticket holders. They listened to his pitch, but baseball wasn't the only leisure activity in the area. Lawson's job required a simple but elusive exchange—money for tickets or advertising. It was a task at which Lawson was a novice and his predecessor, Lyons, was an expert.

Lawson was in charge of Jamestown's front office and Tony Lupien returned to the Falcons as manager. After finishing second with the Falcons in 1951 and winning the Governors Cup in 1952, Lupien had differences with Detroit management and was released. Lupien managed Corning of the PONY League in 1953, but his wife passed away and he resigned halfway into the season. Lupien moved back to his home state of Vermont and spent the 1954 season out of baseball. In 1955, Lupien remarried and was hired back by the Tigers to manage the Falcons. When the season began, he and his second wife were expecting their first child together.

Lupien's return, unfortunately, did not translate into a successful season on the field or in the stands. Detroit provided Jamestown fans with a poor ballclub and the Falcons of Lupien fell to seventh place after a deceptively fast start. The Falcons finished the season only two games out of last place with a record of 48 wins and 78 losses. Only 32,700 came to the park for Lawson, by far the lowest in Jamestown's PONY League history to that point.

At the end of the 1955 season, Detroit put the Jamestown and the Buffalo franchises up for sale. Several deals fell through during the off-season before Lawson and an owner of the local bowling alley turned in an offer they felt was far too low to command serious attention from the Tigers' front office. Detroit immediately accepted the offer, which was reportedly $45,000 less than what they paid Jachym in 1949. Lawson was now the co-owner of the Jamestown Falcons after only one season as general manager. As his first act as owner, Lawson negotiated a new working agreement with the Tigers to continue providing players for the 1956 Falcons.

Soon after the sale of the Falcons to Lawson, Hyde met with Lupien at Dartmouth College, where the three-time Falcons manager was hired to coach baseball. (Lupien was hired, by coincidence, to replace Bob Shawkey—the same man he replaced as Falcons manager in 1951.) In Lupien's New Hampshire office, Hyde and Lupien discussed the distinct changes that had taken place in the minors since the end of the war.

"Television came along and proved to be the straw that broke the camel's back," said Lupien. "Now the really big names people had read and heard about parade through their living room. Why go to the local ballpark when they could turn a switch and see the stars on video."

When the 1956 season began, Jess Queen became the first black professional ballplayer to play for a Jamestown club since the Celoron Acme Colored Giants folded. The Giants were the last blacks to play in organized baseball until Jackie Robinson in 1947, but they were not the first to play for a Jamestown team. There was at least one black player for Jamestown before Harry Curtis' doomed Giants and his name was Richard Andrew (R. A.) Kelly.

First baseman R.A. Kelley was the only black player on the 1890 club called the Jamestowns, and perhaps in the entire Pennsylvania-New York League. Kelley was a barber in Plainfield, Illinois whose baseball skills were noticed by "Big

Sam" Thompson, one of the most feared batters of his day and a future Hall of Famer who played for the 1887 World Champion Detroit Wolverines. In 1889, Thompson and Kelley played in Danville, Illinois of the Illinois-Indiana League, Kelley hitting .317 in his first year of professional ball.

In 1890, five years before Honus Wagner's rookie season and eight years before the Giants played at Celoron, Kelley came to Jamestown. Under general manager Herbert Whitney Tew, Kelley and his teammates played their games at Marvin Park, near Jamestown's boat landing. West of Washington Street, Marvin Park was also used as a horse racing track. Because of its location, the field was subject to the rise and fall of the water level. By mid-season, the field's condition would become so poor that arrangements were made for the town's dam to be opened to lower the outlet water and drain the field.

The *Jamestown Evening Journal* announced the season opener scheduled for May 12, 1890. "Everyone who can leave business and who is fond of the national game, will next Thursday attend the opening of the league season by the Jamestowns and the Oleans on Marvin Park." The water level was high, however, and the game was rescheduled for the next day.

Postponements were common, and it would soon become difficult for fans to know if games were going to be played. The solution was that a flag was hoisted by the *Evening Journal* over their offices in the town's center when games were on. If the flag was down, the scheduled game had been canceled.

The Olean club was greeted at the train station, escorted to the center of town by a large group of Jamestown fans, and took quarters at a hotel called the Humphrey House. "Jamestown people are loyal to the home club, but will always give the visitors a royal welcome," read the *Evening Journal.* Street cars ran every 10 minutes from Third Street to Marvin Park after 3 p.m. and music was played prior to the game. More than 1,500 fans came to Marvin Park to see Jamestown's first professional ballclub win their first game. The crowd also saw Jamestown's first home run, a drive by Kelley off of a pitcher whose last name was Agan and whose first name is unknown.

"Kelley meandered up to the oyster," wrote the *Evening Journal.* "After looking over Agan's assortment of curves he fitted one to the end of his bat and with a simple twist of the wrist dropped it over the right field fence, beside the Tippecanoe log cabin. The spectators stretched their vocal chords and cheered until the knots fell out of the grandstand siding, while Kelley single-footed it around the bases." Kelley was given a new hat for hitting the first homer at Marvin Park, what would be his only one of the season.

Kelley hit .301, with 21 doubles and three triples, to help the Jamestowns take the Pennsylvania-New York league lead on June 3 and hang on for the rest of the season. They clinched the pennant on September 10 with a win in Erie. When Kelley and his teammates arrived home, a reception of 100 fans, a brass band, and firecrackers met them at the train station to accompany them through town. There were no league playoffs, so Kelley's 1890 team was the first Jamestown club to win a league championship.

Kelley returned in 1891 to play for the Jamestowns again. The 1891 Pennsylvania-New York League's second season was split in half—Erie won the first half and Jamestown won the second. The Jamestowns folded at the close of the season, presumably due to financial losses, and Marvin Park was allowed to deteriorate beyond repair. Kelley retired from organized baseball and returned to a barber's life in Plainfield, Illinois.

In 1956, Jess Queen hit .301 with 23 stolen bases for the Falcons and was joined by two future major-leaguers, Phil Regan and Robert Leroy Rodgers. Regan, an 18-year-old rookie pitcher from Michigan, was paid a PONY League standard $2 a day meal money and $250 a month in 1956.

Falcons' manager Greg Mulleay at Municipal Stadium in the early 1940s.

George Zimmerman gave the Falcons their first league championship with a ninth-inning grand slam against Olean in the sixth game of the Governors Cup series.

The "pestiferous" Jake Pitler, Olean manager from 1939 to 1943.

Long-time *Post-Journal* sports editor Frank Hyde in front of the grandstand
wall at Municipal Stadium.

Future Hall of Famer Nellie Fox, Falcons' center fielder in 1944.

Municipal Stadium in 1944. "Lefty" Lyle Parkhurst is on the mound.

Bus driver, trainer, and entertainer Jerry Klein.

The 1952 Jamestown Falcons, including catcher Charlie Lau (far left) and manager Tony Lupien (third from the left).

Jamestown native, Irv Noren, as a New York Yankee.

"I remember the first game we went to was in Wellsville, New York," he later recalled. "We walked into a very small clubhouse and there was mud all over the floor. We had to get dressed in shifts. Our manager said, 'Boys, play hard and get out of this league because you got to get into the big leagues.'" Regan would pitch 13 years in the majors, winning 96 games and earning 92 saves. In 1966, he would be named National League Fireman and Comeback Player of the Year. That season, Regan's Los Angeles Dodgers lost in the World Series to the Baltimore Orioles, a team he would later manage.

During his stay in the PONY League, Regan often fired pitches to Falcons' catcher Robert Leroy Rodgers. Known in the majors as "Buck," the catcher would spend nine years in the majors as a catcher for the Dodgers and then the California Angels. Rodgers would begin his managing career in the majors with the Milwaukee Brewers in 1980.

Wayne Blackburn was again taken from his scouting assignment to manage the Falcons after Pat Mullin, their opening day manager, came down with appendicitis. This time Blackburn could not resuscitate the Falcons as he had done in 1954.

Lawson watched his team, his hopes, and his investment crumble. Less than 20 percent of Municipal Stadium's seats were filled with fans. Municipal Stadium was so empty that, from the field, individual voices could be heard speaking in the grandstand. Lawson even argued with Hank Greenberg of the Cleveland Indian front office. Greenberg, Lawson contended, was stealing fans away from the Falcons by sending a mobile ticket office to the Municipal Stadium parking lot to sell tickets to Indians games, three-and-a-half hours away.

At the end of the season, Hamilton and Bradford both withdrew from the league, bringing the PONY down to six teams for the first time since 1943. Still, Lawson and his fellow owners voted at a July meeting to continue league play, despite the most trying times the PONY League had known.

"This breaks my heart," said Judge Allen Bargar, who had come to games consistently throughout the 1940s and early 1950s, as he left his seat in the grandstand in 1956. "I may never come to a game here again." He never did. Bargar, whose favorite all-time Falcons' player was Johnny Newman, would die on July 21, 1959.

As if financial factors and waning interest in local baseball had not closed in on the PONY League enough during the 1956 season, League President Vince McNamara received word that the very name of their league was being challenged; another organization was using the acronym PONY (standing for Preserve Our Nation's Youth) and planned to bring about legal action if the baseball league, whose directors had never gone through the formality of copyrighting the name, didn't come up with a new one. The league directors quickly voted to change the name to the New York-Pennsylvania League (NY-P) to avoid litigation.

For the final game of the season, Lawson held a free night at Municipal Stadium. There was little to gain by trying to sell any more tickets that season. Attendance had dropped in half again—down to a pitiful 19,757. "I've lost everything in this," he told Hyde. "We didn't quit even when friends advised us to; we put everything we had in it and finished the season. It's no one's fault. The fans and the people of Jamestown have been wonderful. It's simply that the world moves on and perhaps we in baseball haven't kept the pace."

The final scheduled game of the season was rained out in Erie. "Outside the rain continued to come down," wrote Hyde. "Umpire Bill James jumped through the door followed by his partner. James shook the water out of his hair. 'We can't play. It's officially canceled.' His simple statement had written finis to something that has been the heartbeat of sports in Jamestown for nearly two decades. The new order, the new way, had moved in. The old order passeth." Lawson signed over the concessions equipment and team bus, the team's the only remaining assets, to the city of Jamestown.

The Falcons were often called the "Class D Baseball Capital of the World" by George Trautman, the head of the National Association, the governing body of the minor leagues; they were the most successful organization in PONY League history—five Governors Cups in 18 years, including nine finals and 13 playoff appearances; they drew more than 100,000 fans four times, their attendance figures unmatched by any other team in the league. And in September of 1956, they no longer existed.

On October 9, 1956, many Jamestown baseball fans flicked on their televisions to watch the Yankees and the Dodgers play in the World Series for the sixth time in 10 years. They watched Yankees outfielder Irv Noren, Dodgers first base coach Jake Pitler, and Dodgers pitcher Sal Maglie. Jamestowners cheered and moaned in their living rooms as Don Larsen made history by throwing a 97-pitch perfect game and the Yankees went on to win the series four games to three.

Since Municipal Stadium was constructed, the horizon never looked bleaker for professional baseball in Jamestown. With Bargar resolved never to return to Municipal Stadium—the park almost named for him—his old partner, Ernest Kessler, stepped back into the baseball picture alone. Kessler contacted officials with the Pittsburgh Pirates, the same organization that took the Baby Bucs away after one season at Celoron because of the park's poor condition. As president of Jamestown Area Baseball, Inc. in 1957, Kessler convinced the Pittsburgh front office to pick up the Falcons for free and run them for as long as they could.

Jack Paepke, a tall, drawling Californian who played on the 1949 Hollywood Stars with John O'Neil and Irv Noren, was named manager of the Jamestown Falcons for 1957. Paepke's 6-foot 4-inch first baseman was Donn Clendennon, who would go to the majors with Pittsburgh and, in mid-season of 1969, be traded to the "Miracle" Mets where he hit three home runs in 14 World Series at-bats.

Despite only slightly less disheartening attendance figures (484 per game in 1957 as opposed to 274 per game in 1956) there was still hope for Paepke's club. Pittsburgh's accountants determined that if Jamestown could draw 1,500 fans for a three-game series in the third week of June, payroll could be met and the club could survive another two weeks. The turnstiles clicked that weekend but still far too infrequently and far too late. The Pirates announced that the final night of the season for Jamestown would be a doubleheader on June 25, "Jamestown Sports Hall of Fame Night." "It's like losing an old friend, but I guess that's the way it has to be," said Kessler. "We had a product for sale—just one product, baseball—and the public didn't want it."

League President Vince McNamara came to pay his respects with Kessler at Municipal Stadium. In between the games of the doubleheader, the "Hall of Fame Night" ceremonies honored two local sports figures, neither baseball players. The Falcons won the first and took a 2-0 lead into the top of the eighth in the second and final game, but gave up two in the bottom of the eighth and four in the ninth to lose 6-4.

"Eighteen hundred turned out for the wake last night," Hyde wrote. "Few probably realize it, but they were also sitting in on the grand finale of minor-league baseball in general. The minors will be gone within five years. The old fiery days of hometown pride, when a man threw out his chest and said, 'this is my town' and the 'our boys' spirit is fading. We've become a nation of whiners, cynics and nonbelievers who demand the ultimate in comfort and performance. Baseball cannot cope with the trend—in Jamestown, Buffalo, or in New York City. Something may change all that—a depression, perhaps, when a sense of values returns to the masses—but as of today, minor-league baseball is fighting a losing battle."

After a last ditch effort to shift the club to Niagara Falls, the Falcons folded. Professional baseball in Jamestown had apparently drawn its final breath.

SEVEN

From LATE JUNE OF 1957 TO MARCH OF 1961, Municipal Stadium remained quiet and still. But the characters who had thrilled Jamestown baseball fans were busy playing for major-league baseball fans across the country. In Brooklyn, 10 days before "Hall of Fame Night" formally ushered professional baseball out of Jamestown in 1957, Greg Mulleavy was called from his managing position in Montreal to coach in Brooklyn. During the second half of the 1957 season—the final season played at Ebbets Field— Mulleavy and his old rival "Jumping" Jake Pitler shared a clubhouse as Dodgers coaches. It was Pitler's final season with the Dodgers, but Mulleavy would go on to Los Angeles the next season. Mulleavy and his family said their good-byes to friends in Jamestown and moved to California before the 1958 season opened.

Mulleavy coached the Dodgers until 1961, when Leo Durocher, the ex-manager of the New York Giants (whose club made it to the World Series in 1951 and 1954) was hired as manager. Mild-mannered Mulleavy didn't get along well with the brusque Durocher and he returned to scouting. In 1960, Irv Noren completed his career with Mulleavy and the Dodgers. Also on the 1961 Dodgers were Bob "Buck" Rodgers and Maury Wills, still haunted by Al Campanis for his late night in Jamestown as a member of Doc Alexson's Hornell club.

In the American League in 1957, Bob Shaw and Charlie Lau were beginning their careers in the major leagues with the Detroit Tigers. Shaw would soon be traded to the White Sox where he and second baseman Nellie Fox would lead their club to a World Series against the Dodgers in 1959. The Dodgers won the series in six games despite Bob Shaw's 1-0 shutout against Sandy Koufax in front of 92,706 fans in Los Angeles, an all-time attendance record for a World Series game. Across Lake Michigan from the losing Chicago White Sox, in Garden City, Michigan, Michael Illitch was putting the finishing touches on his first Little Caesar's restaurant.

In Detroit, Charlie Lau caught for Frank Lary, the "Yankee Killer." When Phil Regan joined the Tigers in 1960, he became the 38th former Jamestown player to make it to the majors, according to Frank Hyde. By the end of the 1960 season, Jamestown players had appeared in nine of the last 12 World Series.

Forty-three years earlier, in 1914, Jamestown had become home to it's first organized baseball team of the 20th century. The team was the first professional ballclub in Jamestown registered with the National Association (a requirement for a club to be considered a part of "organized" baseball) and would be the last until 1939, with the founding of the PONY League.

The Jamestown team was one of six teams in the newly formed Class D Interstate League, a carefully planned league whose directors had high hopes for long-term success. All Sunday and holiday game receipts would be pooled and split evenly among the six clubs and the league's compactness (60 miles was the longest traveling distance) would keep travel costs low. In late April, Niagara Falls' entry was dropped because the other clubs in the league protested the trip north and the increased travel expenses it would bring. Wellsville was substituted as the sixth team in the league and a meeting of local businessmen raised $750 dollars to help put a club on the field.

To prepare for the 1914 season, Celoron Park's grounds were landscaped, its white wooden grandstand was repaired and cleaned, and a concrete arch was erected at the ballpark's entrance. The manager of the Jamestown club, Joe Lohr (as a regular outfielder on the Atlantic League's pennant-winning Reading club), offered a season pass to the fan suggesting the best nickname for the team. Apparently, the prize was never awarded because the team remained nicknameless throughout the 1914 season.

The home opener brought the obligatory parade which started at 2 p.m. in downtown Brooklyn Square. A line of more than 20 automobiles were led by the Eagle Military Band east on Main Street to Washington Street. A proclamation issued by Mayor Samuel A. Carlson closed a number of stores and offices so employees could celebrate professional baseball in Jamestown. At Celoron Park, after the Jamestowns and the visiting Warren Bingos went through batting and fielding practice, the players of both teams gathered in center field, formed a line the width of the playing field, and marched to the grandstand. Mayor Carlson threw out the ceremonial first pitch of the season.

The Warren club had beaten Jamestown 10-7 the day before in the season opener in Warren. Dressed in blue and white uniforms, Jamestown lost their home opener and dropped a game the next night to start the season 0-3. Despite early domination by Warren, a season-long rivalry developed between the two cities. Warren manager Billy "The Rabbit" Webb, who had been a third baseman for several

Jamestown semi-pro teams, helped spark some of the tension between the Jamestown team and the Bingos.

In 1910, Webb and five other ballplayers came from Philadelphia to Jamestown to try out with a local semi-pro team managed by a man named Hugh Shannon. After spending a few days in town, Webb and the others were turned away without getting a chance to demonstrate their skills. But at the station waiting for their train home, the secretary of the semi-pro club stopped them and asked them to wait for the next train. Meanwhile, the team's directors were holding a meeting to fire manager Shannon and offer the job to Frank Corneal, one of the six Philadelphia ballplayers. Corneal took the job and signed the other five. Webb played with Jamestown semi-pro teams from 1910 to 1913, then was hired to manage the Warren Bingos.

Another factor in the rivalry between Warren and Jamestown was pitcher Ralph Davie, a semi-pro player in Warren in 1913 who stayed in town to begin the 1914 season as a Bingo. In the third game of the year, Davie pitched a 9-3 complete game win (helped by the fact that all but two Jamestown starters made errors). Midway through the season, however, Davie left Warren and joined the Jamestown club.

On September 14, two days after The Sons of Veterans celebrated the 100th anniversary of the composition of "The Star Spangled Banner" by Francis Scott Key, and almost four months after he pitched Warren to a victory over Jamestown, Davie beat the Bingos in the final game of the season at Celoron. He threw a four-hit complete game, his only mistake a home run ball hit to deep center.

Jamestown won the first half of the season and the Bradford (Pa.) Drillers won the second half, setting up a best-of-seven playoff series for the league championship. Lohr's Jamestowners won the opener 6-4 in Bradford. In the second game, also in Bradford, Ralph Davie started and pitched well until a nightmarish fifth inning. "By the time three Drillers had been retired, 12 men had faced Davie, nine runs had crossed the plate between a fusillade of seven safe swats, including three triples and a pugilistic encounter between [Jamestown] catcher Mulvoy and Umpire Cleary," read the *Jamestown Evening Journal*.

"The altercation between Mulvoy and Cleary occurred when the latter called [Bradford's catcher] Clark safe on a close play. Mulvoy took a punch at the umpire but before the affair went any further the battlers were separated and Mulvoy was banished from the game. Manager Lohr however had no substitute to put in and so after a discussion that lasted over a half an hour Mulvoy was allowed to return and the game was continued. After the long delay, Davie cooled off but never got back into form. The game was called at the end of the eighth because of darkness. Bradford won 11-3 to tie the series at one."

Jamestown and Bradford split the next four games, meaning the deciding game seven would be played in Bradford on Saturday, September 26. Davie threw a complete game shutout and Jamestown won their first National Association-recognized league championship.

When the series was over, Warren manager Billy Webb organized an Interstate All-Star team composed of players from the Interstate League, Canadian League, International League, and State League in order to continue playing in late September and early October.

Their second game was played against a local semi-pro team, Art Metal Fire Brigade, with their guest pitcher and New York Highlander Ray Caldwell. "It was a loosely played battle," read the *Evening Journal*, "but had the desired result, that is, a chance for the fans to see the All-Stars in action as well as 'Slim' Caldwell." By the time Caldwell came in as a reliever in the fifth inning, the score was 14-8. Caldwell faced the All-Stars' lineup of center fielder Lohr and third baseman Webb while Davie watched from the dugout on his night off. Caldwell allowed just three hits and one run in four innings but the All-Stars won 15-8.

In the majors, future Jamestown Falcons manager Bob Shawkey started the fourth game of the World Series for Connie Mack's Philadelphia A's against the Boston Braves. Shawkey gave up three runs in five innings to get the loss, which also concluded a four-game sweep by the Braves.

During the off-season, Jamestown's 1914 manager, Joe Lohr, was hired to manage Wellsville. With the season fast approaching, it looked as if Jamestown would be without a team. Webb, who was still under contract to Warren, was Jamestown's only hope.

On March 4, 1915, the *Evening Journal* carried this report: "It will be welcome news to baseball fans in this city today to learn that Billy Webb has been signed up to manage the Jamestown club during the coming season. Warren realized that the life of the league depended upon Jamestown's action and after considering the matter came across with the desired papers. Webb, who had already signed the entire Warren team, immediately began to comb the surrounding country for new men."

"Well," said Webb to the *Evening Journal*, "you can tell the fans for me that this town will be represented by a ballclub this year, that's for certain. Of course, I'm not saying that it will be a pennant winner because baseball's mighty uncertain, but it will be a club that can play baseball and I'll see that Jamestown gets just as high class all this year as last, if not a little better. . . Just between you and I, this is my hometown now," Webb said of Jamestown. "I know all the fans here and I'm glad Warren was good enough to let me come back." In Webb's honor, the 1915 Jamestown team was nicknamed "The Rabbits."

One of Webb's signings in 1915 was Leon Carlson, a 20-year-old Jamestown pitcher. Carlson would make it to the majors in 1920 as a teammate of Erik "Swat" Erickson, another Jamestown pitcher, with the Washington Senators. Carlson only pitched three games for the Senators, his time in the majors cut short because he couldn't field his position well. "I never could master it, so I quit," he said of his fielding inability.

The first of Carlson's three major-league appearances was against the Yankees at the Polo Grounds. He came in to relieve Walter Johnson who was having a rare off day. "What a greenhorn I was," he later recalled to Hyde. "They called me in from the bullpen—my first big league appearance. I was so scared I started to walk in real slow, then some bull-voiced fan in the upper tier yelled, 'Run, you jughead, run.' So what did I do? Why I ran to the huge delight of the crowd." When Carlson reached the mound, he looked to the plate and saw Babe Ruth waiting for a delivery.

"Brick Owens was umpiring behind the plate," Carlson continued. "He walked out, looked at me intently for a moment, and asked: 'Scared?' 'Brick,' I replied. 'I'm so scared I don't even know where the ball is going.' Owens laughed and said, 'You're to be commended for admitting it.'"

Then Carlson's catcher, Val Picinich, came out to the mound. "Know who that is up there?" the catcher asked, spitting a long stream of tobacco juice. "Well, keep it down and away from him. Make him hit it on the ground. Don't try to strike him out."

Carlson toed the rubber and fired home. Ruth swung and missed. The next pitch was a ball, followed by another swinging strike. Then Carlson tossed a pitch right down the middle of the plate and Ruth took it for strike three. "Strrrike!" roared Owens. Carlson had struck out Ruth on four pitches. "The buttons were bursting right off my shirt when I went to the dugout," Carlson remembered. "'So that's Babe Ruth?' I asked. 'Yeah, stick around long enough and you'll get acquainted,' someone drawled." Two days later, Carlson again came in to face Ruth in the late innings of a game at the Polo Grounds. "I gave him one low and outside as Picinich advised before," Carlson said. "Ruth let it go, dug in a little, and waited. I came in with another one, a little higher. Ruth swung. It was gone. That was the longest homer I ever saw."

In 1914, Carlson was with Webb's Rabbits and took the mound in front of 1,400 Jamestown fans for opening day against Warren. A pennant reading "Champions of the Interstate League for 1914" flew just below the American flag in center field. Carlson gave up only six hits and three runs while pitching through a light drizzle, and the Rabbits beat the Bingos 6-3.

The most eagerly awaited games in 1915 were against Wellsville, managed by Joe Lohr and featuring former Jamestown ace pitcher Ralph Davie. (Wellsville would go on to win the league with a 54-32 record.) More than 2,000 fans filled Celoron Park when Wellsville came to town and they rode Lohr hard as the Rabbits won 3-2. "Everything was taken in the proper spirit however," read the *Evening Journal*, "and the fans gave Lohr credit for losing like a prince."

Midway through the season, Harry Josiah "Buggs" Eccles joined the Rabbits to strengthen their pitching staff. An 18-year-old southpaw from the neighboring town of Kennedy, Eccles was coming off of a short stay with the 1915 Philadelphia Athletics. Eccles appeared in just five games for the A's, starting one and totaling an 0-1 record in 21 innings pitched. Unfortunately for Eccles, both the A's and the Rabbits were last-place clubs in 1915. Under manager Connie Mack, the A's were one of the worst major-league teams of all time and finished with a 43-109 record. The Rabbits weren't too far behind, on their way to a 28-42 record.

A break in the 1915 action came on August 8 when Eric "Swat" Erickson, in the midst of his lemon-helped miracle season, and his Rochester Hustlers stopped at Celoron for an exhibition game. Erickson struck out nine and gave up only five hits, but made a costly error in the first inning when he dropped the ball trying to cover first base, and the Hustlers lost to the Rabbits 3-2. Unfortunately, the crowd was limited to less than 1,000 due to heavy rain throughout the game.

After the Hustlers left that evening, three of Webb's players quit the Rabbits because they, like their teammates, had not yet received a month's worth of back pay. "It was hoped that with a good day Sunday and with Rochester as the attraction a large crowd would turn out and the gate receipts would greatly aid in pulling the team out of its financial trouble," reported the *Evening Journal*. "As had generally been known, several of the players had declined offers from other teams in the hope that they would receive some of their back pay on Sunday. The poor crowd made this impossible and this morning [first baseman] Servatius, [center fielder] Lindholm, and [second baseman] Getzie left the team."

Webb said he would try to continue with local players but two days later, on August 10, he resigned when he realized the seriousness of the team's financial troubles. "Few fans in this city realize the problem that has been before the directors to keep the team," read the *Evening Journal*. "When the team is playing on the road the guarantee given by the home clubs provides enough to allow the team to break even but as has been the case during the entire summer, games have been continually called off on account of rain. Thus the team on every road trip has been losing money due to the continuous rain which has caused serious losses to nearly every baseball team in the country."

Fingers were quickly pointed, most often at the Interstate League's President Lindsey for not taking action earlier. "The matter was put up to him about three weeks ago and at that time he did not seem to care whether Jamestown remained in the league or dropped out," the *Evening Journal* reported. "A meeting was called at Olean, the Jamestown club refused any financial assistance, and its representatives were sent home with the same directions. 'Try again.'"

With three weeks remaining, Jamestown's club withdrew from the league. "While the league may keep on its feet with five clubs," said Lindsey, "the action of Jamestown is going to cripple and inconvenience the circuit to an alarming extent. It has remained for the largest city in the league to lay down on the job and let its team die through apathy and lack of support."

Forty-two years later, Ernest Kessler refused to give up on professional baseball and the ballpark he had helped build, even after the miserable failure of the Pirates' ownership in 1957. Each off-season, Kessler contacted major-league executives with which he was acquainted. Letters were returned like one from the Phillies sent in the winter of 1958: "We had hoped to come to Jamestown in 1959, but since there was little action right now in your city we decided on a one-year working agreement with Elmira."

Kessler negotiated with Pittsburgh farm director Branch Rickey Jr. (Branch Rickey Sr. had since retired) in January of 1959. "Jamestown, N.Y. is available and it is one of the finest franchises in the United States," Rickey Jr. wrote in a letter to the sports editor of the *Tallahassee Democrat.* "There is, of course, a problem of whether Jamestown can pay off the liens against the franchise, organize a corporation and sell sufficient tickets in time to operate this year." Rickey Jr. and the Pirates organization decided against the risk and Kessler went back to his list of phone numbers and addresses.

Kessler's break came when Hillman Lyons returned to Jamestown. After leaving Jamestown to be general manager of the Buffalo Bisons, Lyons moved on to Charleston, West Virginia in 1956. His 1958 team drew 160,000 and won the pennant but the gifted salesman felt there was little chance for further advancement in baseball and took an offer with the International Hotel chain and was given the assignment of running the Hotel Jamestown starting January 4, 1960.

"I feel that having a baseball club in the city is as essential as the possession of a hotel," Lyons said when he returned. Kessler and Lyons called on friends in the Detroit Tigers' front office and drew the Tigers back into a working agreement with Jamestown in the late winter of 1961. Professional baseball, in the form of the Jamestown Tigers, was back.

Under this new arrangement, the team was owned and operated by a group of local Jamestowners led by Kessler, who would try to keep baseball going at Municipal Stadium. Detroit would provide the players, managers, coaches, trainers, and baseball equipment. This arrangement—a major-league club handling baseball operations and local interests running the front office—would continue for the next 13 years.

"Now it's up to the fans," wrote Hyde just prior to the scheduled home opener at Municipal Stadium. "How the fruits of their labors will react on the masses remains to be seen," he said of Lyon's and Kessler's efforts. Unfortunately, the elements were unfriendly on opening day, 1961. Three-hundred Jamestowners huddled for warmth in the Municipal Stadium grandstand while biting winds swirled and freezing rain threatened to turn to snow. "In the Good Old Summertime," a song already dated in 1961, crackled over the PA system and brought a lighthearted tone to the bitter-cold evening. When the song ended, it was announced that the game was canceled.

Three days later, on another cold but this time clear night in Jamestown, about 1,600 fans came out to see the Tigers play. "Municipal Stadium looked as green and lovely as a piece of Erin," wrote a *Post-Journal* reporter named Jerry Scorse. "The smells of popcorn, peanuts and hot dogs; the young holding hands and the old holding coffee. And the ballplayers feeling as young ballplayers do, the relief of playing before a friendly, home audience; and the dejection that comes sometimes with letting the home folk down. Because, you see, it was swell again at the ballyard last night."

Jamestown beat Elmira 9-7, but it was the base umpire, "Lefty" Lyle Parkhurst, who stole the show. "You're blind, ump!" screamed a fan when a visiting Elmira base runner dove headfirst to beat a pick-off throw. Parkhurst—the local boy who threw back-to-back shutouts on the final two days of the 1944 season—called him safe and Jamestown fans let him know they didn't like the call. John Newman, Parkhurst's former teammate, sat quietly in the stands as did "Swat" Erickson.

"The home team won, the umpires were knaves, the bleacherites yelled the loudest," wrote Hyde in his column the next day. "And Jamestown was better off than Brooklyn—we had a pro ball team again, to love, cherish, honor and hooray, until too many losses do us part."

Lyons must have read the *Post-Journal* column with delight, but knew the process of selling baseball in Jamestown was a perpetual one. There were contests and lucky numbers and promotional nights, like the appearance of Hardrock Simpson, a 56-year-old man who was paid to run along the periphery of baseball fields from the first pitch to the final out. "I like to run—been doin' it for 50 years," he told Hyde. "Let the people sit. I like to run so I thought up this thing to turn it into money." Hyde added, "Hardrock belongs to a fading generation that caters to the bizarre. At heart he's a flagpole sitter, a mountain climber, a man who bites the heads off snakes or rides a motorcycle around a den of lions."

The fans came to the ballpark that season. In 1961, Lyons' team led the league in attendance by more than 25,000 fans. By mid-June, fans had bought 2,107 hot dogs, 300 bags of peanuts, 300 ice cream bars, 120 cigars, and 946 soft drinks. "We were out of some things before our first game was over," remarked Lyons.

That season, a bench-clearing brawl broke out between the Tigers and the visiting Corning club. Players raced to the field and the umpires struggled to separate them one-by-one. Jerry Klein, Jamestown trainer and bus driver, called up to the press box from the grandstand rows where he was selling programs and told the PA announcer to play "The Star Spangled Banner" to calm the players. The PA announcer raced to find the record but, in his haste to slap it on the player, the record shattered. He yelled back down to tell Klein what had happened and the rumble on the field continued. Klein ran to the staircase at the rear of the grandstand and climbed to the press box, pausing only to drop the pile of programs he had been carrying. He arrived at the microphone out of breath and sweating, but began singing the national anthem anyway as several spectators were making their way out to the field to add to the chaos. The fight subsided due to Klein's hoarse and out of breath singing and to the presence of police officers who came out to the field to break up the remaining brawlers. One Corning player who fought to the end was asked why he kept throwing punches during the anthem. "I thought someone got hurt and was groaning in pain!"

The 1961 Jamestown Tigers were led by manager Al Federoff, a former Falcons second baseman who played in Jamestown in 1945 and 1947. Federoff played with Detroit in 1951, where he hit .242, scored 14 runs, and had 14 RBIs. A rookie in 1945, Federoff was middleman in the Koshorek-to-Federoff-to-Alexson double play combination that at one time averaged two double plays per game for 21 consecutive games.

"Jamestown Sports Hall of Fame Night" was also revived at Municipal Stadium in 1961, held at the second-to-last home game of the season. The Tigers were stuck in sixth place, which made the game of little importance, but the crowd was large and enthusiastic. The evening opened with a home run derby, then followed by a race around the base paths which was won by Tigers catcher Ralph Woods. After the race, Woods grabbed a microphone and sang "If I Loved You." The crowd went wild at the catcher's smooth voice, accompanied by organist Margaret Miller. Two local sports figures—a bowler and a football coach—were inducted into the local Hall of Fame and Jamestown outfielder Jim Rooker hit five singles in five at-bats to help beat the visiting Auburn club.

Soon after the 1961 season ended, an auction was held at Municipal Stadium to raise funds for professional baseball in Jamestown. More than 1,000 townspeople showed up to bid for the services of almost 200 civic leaders and prominent citizens who offered themselves up as "Slaves of Baseball." Two city leaders brought in $10 apiece to play badminton barefoot at Municipal Stadium on New Year's Day. The mayor and the police chief commanded $65 and $55, respectively, to wait on customers at a local Italian restaurant. One Jamestowner paid $10 to receive personal service by Hillman Lyons at the Hotel Jamestown cocktail lounge. That night, Lyons was also named "Sports Man of the Year" by the local media for bringing professional baseball back to Jamestown.

"Slaves of Baseball" ensured the return of baseball in 1962. That meant that in the spring, Frank Hyde would be at the Detroit Tigers' spring training facility in Lakeland, Florida. Hyde noted that the former Air Force base had taken on even more of a military feel since his last visit there 15 years earlier. "Scouting is more thorough and training conditions are better," he wrote. "Efficiency" was the new buzz-word in baseball. "It costs us about $9 per day to carry a player here," a Detroit official said. Hyde observed that every dollar and player was accounted for, and a successful organization was one in which the highest possible number of players advanced from the lower minors to the majors in as short a time as possible.

Detroit's front office claimed that the Jamestown club, to be managed by Frank "Stubby" Overmire, would have excellent speed and offer baseball comparable to Class C (a full step above the Class D NY-P League). Overmire was an ex-major-league pitcher and a member of the 1945 World Series champion Detroit Tigers along with former Jamestown Falcons' catcher Russell Kerns and Jerry Lawson's front office nemesis from Cleveland, Hank Greenberg. Overmire started game three, pitched six innings, and gave up only two earned runs. Unfortunately, his club was shut out and lost the game 3-0.

Overmire pitched more than 200 innings during three different seasons and once threw a two-hitter against the Chicago White Sox. He managed four minor-league clubs between 1955 and 1960, including two pennant winners. Overmire lived with his wife and two children in Grand Rapids, Michigan, where he worked in a varnish factory during the off-season.

"How about ballplayers?" Hyde asked Overmire. "Are young players different than years ago?"

"Yes, there is less desire," the Jamestown Tigers' manager answered, a comment managers have apparently always made about the younger generation of players. "But there is still the boy who wants to play and the boy who don't give a hang. It doesn't take long to weed them out."

Jim Rooker was one player who did "give a hang." He was an outfielder for the Falcons in 1961, but returned to Jamestown in 1962 as a pitcher. During the off-season, Tigers' coaches made the wise decision to try him out on the mound. Rooker would make it all the way to the majors as a pitcher, spending eight of his thirteen years in the majors with the Pittsburgh Pirates, including an appearance in the 1979 World Series.

In 1962, the Tigers were in first place for a total of only 29 days of the 120-game regular season but they pulled ahead of Erie in mid-August and won the NY-P pennant, as predicted by Detroit. A telegram came to Hyde at the *Post-Journal* building from Detroit's vice president the morning after Overmire's team clinched the pennant: "Jamestown's championship proved we were right in spring training when we told Stubby that he'd be laughing all the way to the pennant."

Detroit's gloating was cut short, however, when the Mets defeated the Tigers in two straight games in a best-of-three semi-final series. "We are pooped," Overmire said. "I guess both Jamestown and Erie beat each other over the head too much in the pennant race."

Of a more immediate concern to Jamestowners was that Hillman Lyons was becoming unavoidably preoccupied with his position at the Hotel Jamestown and had to distance himself from everyday baseball operations. Two Jamestown sports figures, Marty Haines and Russ Diethrick, stepped in and took control of the Jamestown Tigers' front office. Haines was a quick-quipping businessman who rose to prominence in the Jamestown sports scene as secretary for the area's active bowling association. During the 1950s, he spent over a year in Europe trying to promote the sport of bowling for the Professional Bowlers Association. "It sounded good," he later commented dead-pan, "but it just didn't work out."

Diethrick was literally born with baseball. His father had been a coal miner in Central Pennsylvania and his mother, while pregnant with Russ, would write down the box scores of the ballgames off of the radio while his father worked. His mother's due date drew nearer as Branch Rickey's St. Louis Cardinals, with Leo Durocher at shortstop, faced Hank Greenberg and the Detroit Tigers in the 1934 World Series. Russ was born on October 9 and the Cardinals beat the Tigers later that day.

When he was five, the local coal mine closed down and his family moved to Jamestown. He was six when Municipal Stadium was christened and ten when Parkhurst tossed his two shutouts. He grew up watching and playing baseball with friends in the lots and fields of his town, often in the snow or in the dark. Towards the end of his teenage years, still interested in baseball as a player and an umpire, he took a job at a local factory where he would cross paths with young Flo White. He worked alongside John O'Neil and Duane Shaffer—the men he had watched at Municipal Stadium as a child. Like Ernest Kessler, Diethrick became recognized for his integrity and his ability to get things done. When Kessler and Lyons reorganized the club in 1961, Diethrick was a board member.

As leaders of Jamestown Furniture City Baseball, Diethrick and Haines named John O'Neil general manager of the Tigers. Since O'Neil's second stint as Falcon's shortstop in 1954, he general managed at Valdosta, Georgia from 1955 to 1958 (Overmire was his field manager in a pennant-winning 1958 season) and Montgomery in 1959. After that, O'Neil scouted for the Detroit Tigers until he was offered the job by

Diethrick and Haines in 1963.

Also that off-season, the operators of the National Association and Major League Baseball decided upon a new "Player Development Plan." A new classification system was devised in which the old A, B, C, D, and Rookie system was replaced with AAA, AA, A, and Rookie (in declining order of competitiveness). For Jamestown, it meant that the NY-P was a Class A League, though little change in the caliber of players was anticipated by Detroit.

O'Neil's first season as general manager, and Overmire's second as field manager, began in the familiar cold wind and rain of recent NY-P opening weeks. But Jamestown's pitching staff, including future major-leaguers Pat Dobson, Jack DiLauro, and John Hiller, threw like it was the middle of July. Twenty-one-year-old right-hander Pat Dobson, who fanned nineteen for the Tigers early in the summer, would spend eleven seasons in the majors. He would win ten or more games seven times, including a 20-8 season with Baltimore in 1971 and two World Series appearances.

Nineteen-year-old southpaw Jack DiLauro was 14-10 in 1963. "Left-handers are supposed to be crazy, mixed up kids like goat stew who throw with scatter-gun arms," wrote Hyde of the big boyish-faced pitcher from Akron after DiLaura's seventh win lifted Jamestown into third place on June 22. "The Ohio Kid is changing all that." Hyde noted that DiLauro only walked 20 men through 75 innings. He would go on to play for the Mets in the 1969 World Series with 1957 Jamestown first basemen Donn Clendennon. Twenty-year-old left-hander John Hiller was 14-9 in 1963. That season, Hiller would earn 38 saves and win Fireman of the Year as best reliever in the NY-P League. The Toronto-born Hiller would pitch for 15 years in the majors and compile a lifetime 87-76 record, mostly in relief, and all with the Tigers.

The 1963 Jamestown Tigers didn't stay together as a group very long. On June 3, Dobson and the team's leading hitter, Wilbert Franklin, were promoted to Detroit's class AA affiliate in Knoxville, Tennessee. Two weeks later, the Tigers were on the road in Geneva when Overmire was awakened by the ring of his hotel room phone. Detroit's front office had decided that Overmire was needed with the major-league Tigers in Boston. Travel arrangements were quickly made. He packed his bags, retrieved his belongings from the team bus, and took a cab to Rochester where he rented a car. Overmire arrived in Jamestown just before 4 a.m., emptied his apartment, and hopped a flight to Boston. He arrived at Fenway, with plenty of time to spare, before the Tigers' game against the Red Sox that night. From his Boston hotel room after the game, Overmire called Hyde. "I had to move fast and I don't want anyone to think I ran out without a word," Overmire told him. "Those Jamestown fans have been great to me."

Though the fans were kind to Overmire, they were growing frustrated with the constant shuffling of players that was becoming standard practice in organized baseball. A fan could no longer assume that a player that came to Jamestown in April would still be there in September.

"Jamestown fans should not be too critical of Detroit," wrote Hyde in his column. "In the past when communities carried the load—paid the salaries, spring training, etc.—parent organizations seldom moved popular players or managers during the season. As hometown interest faded, minor-league operators leaned more and more on the parent organizations for financial and player support. Now they pay the freight. It is only natural that they call the turn."

The Tigers finished in fourth place without Overmire and qualified for a best-of-three semi-finals against pennant-winner Wellsville. The Tigers won two out of three in the semi-finals to qualify for a best-of-three finals against Batavia.

The Tigers took the first game on the road, but dropped the second, setting up one winner-take-all game at Municipal Stadium for the Governors Cup of the NY-P League. On a comfortable September Saturday night, only 687 Jamestowners watched the Tigers lose 7-3.

The 1964 Jamestown Tigers were a mediocre club which would finish in fourth place and attract little attention from Jamestown baseball fans. They were managed by Jack Phillips—a part-time first baseman for the Yankees in the 1940s and former teammate of Clem Koshorek's in Pittsburgh—and played in the renamed "College Stadium." The name "Municipal Stadium" was abandoned as a result of the construction of Jamestown Community College in a large plot of land beyond the ballpark's right field.

That season, general manager John O'Neil and the city bus drivers made plans for a "John Newman Night" at College Stadium. Newman, who had just been released from the local hospital where he suffered from a weight-related illness, would receive all proceeds to help pay his medical bills. "Newman did for the PONY League what Babe Ruth did for the majors," his former teammate O'Neil said. "Now we hope the fans will turn out to show their appreciation."

Two of Newman's former teammates from the 1941 club remembered Newman's home runs years later. When Municipal Stadium was opened, it was Falcons pitcher Dick Schmidt who threw the first official pitch (a strike) to catcher Johnny Pollock. Schmidt and Pollock both stayed in Jamestown after their playing days were done. Schmidt recalled that Newman hit a home run in 1941 that cleared the light standard in left field "by at least 15 feet." Two fans outside the park claimed they stepped off the distance from the 340-foot mark at the left field fence and estimated the ball had traveled 600 feet on the fly.

Pollock was not only the starting catcher at Municipal Stadium's inaugural game in 1941; he was also the opening day catcher at Celoron Park in 1939 for the Jamestown Baby Bucs. Pollock went with the Baby Bucs to London, Ontario in 1940, then signed with Bisgeier for the 1941 season which returned him to Jamestown. Pollock also played for the

Falcons in 1946, sharing the catching duties with Russ Kerns. In fact, it was Pollock's injury—a hit on the head—that forced Marv Olson to put Clem Koshorek into the lineup at third base. Pollock married a local girl and stayed in Jamestown, where he and O'Neil would remain golf buddies for decades.

Pollock remembered his teammate, John Newman, years later. "He was a gentleman's gentleman," Pollock said. "Sure, I recall his great hitting, but I'd rather talk about John Newman, the man."

The 1964 "John Newman Night" preceded a mid-season Tigers game at College Stadium and began with an old-timers band and baton twirling demonstration. Newman took his place at home plate, where he had been presented a key to the city as part of the original "John Newman Night" in 1942. Season ticket holders paid twice for their tickets as a donation for Newman, and former teammates Schmidt, Pollock, and O'Neil all cheered for him from the grandstand. Despite the community's support, Newman lived just three more years. He died in 1967.

With the exception of Newman's tribute, there was so little interest in the 1964 season that Diethrick, Haines, and O'Neil concurred with Wellsville management's suggestion that the semi-final series scheduled between their teams not even be played. Cutting losses seemed to be the wisest decision. As was becoming a year-end tradition, Diethrick and his partners met at the close of the season to add up Jamestown Furniture's total debt. The monetary amount was divided evenly and personal checks were written by each to cover their losses.

Low community interest and profits opened the door for unwelcome consultants such as "Minor League Troubleshooter" Warren LaTarte, whose pouty lips and hanging cheeks made him look like a droop-faced dog. LaTarte worked for the National Association and it was his job to attend league and club meetings where he was to lis-

ten and offer suggestions on management strategies and promotions. He arrived in Jamestown during the late winter of
1965.

"Don't forget, baseball has a new look today," said
LaTarte at a meeting with Diethrick, Hyde, and the rest of
Jamestown Furniture. "The records prove it. Today's Class A
ballplayer has something else in his hip pocket—a college
diploma—and something under his hat—brains." He paused for
a breath. "Special nights, gimmicks, a show for the fans—and
publicity!"

LaTarte's suggestions were not all well-received by Diethrick
and Haines who had to deal with the reality of running a
club on an ever-tightening budget. According to Hyde,
when LaTarte didn't like what the Jamestown Furniture
representatives had to say, "[He] squirmed like a fellow sitting
on a cocklebur."

LaTarte wasn't necessarily wrong. Changes did need to be
made by the Jamestown Furniture management. After the
Lyons-inspired 1961 and 1962 seasons, in which attendance
averaged more than 65,000 fans a year, O'Neil's efforts in
1963 and 1964 went unrewarded and attendance shrunk in
half to 31,360 and 34,121, respectively. Haines decided to try
taking over as general manager himself.

As general manager, Haines started fast. He converted his
local bowling and sports connections into a generous
"green stamp" promotion from the local Quality Markets
grocery store chain. With little pizzazz but much practical
allure, 6,000 stamps, good for purchases at a participating
store, would be distributed to fans at every Jamestown
Tigers home game. Haines also announced an opening day
program that included an appearance by Miss Chautauqua
County to "Cut the Tigers loose by snipping a ribbon,"
according to a press release announcing the event. John
Pollock would also be on hand to receive a pitch from the
former Falcons pitcher Dick Schmidt, a reenactment of the
first pitch at Municipal Stadium. In addition, according to

Detroit's front office, Jamestown would have a strong club in 1965.

"Tigers will win in NY-P League," said Detroit farm director Don Lund, an outfielder with the Dodgers, Cardinals, and Tigers in the late 1940s and early 1950s. "That's my prediction and you can quote me that way in the *Post-Journal*."

The Tigers finished dead last. Jim Leyland, who later managed the Pittsburgh Pirates and the Florida Marlins, was back-up catcher. Due to the all-too-frequent blow-outs the Tigers suffered in 1965, Leyland was given the opportunity to pitch occasionally. "I was not a prospect so, in case someone hurts their arm, at least you're not hurting the arm of someone pretty good," recalled Leyland.

One weekend series against the league-leading Binghamton Triplets summed up the 1965 Tigers season. On Saturday night, the outmatched Tigers played 21 innings of tie baseball with the Triplets until Jamestown's 1 a.m. curfew forced the game to be replayed the next day as the first of a doubleheader. Leyland and the Tigers' manager, Gail Henley, were both thrown out for arguing a close call at the plate during the first game, which the Tigers lost 2-0. They lost the second 12-1. When the weekend was over, the Falcons had played 39 innings, sustained a stretch of 19 scoreless innings, and added two more losses to their last place record.

"I'm shocked that the club fared so badly," Detroit assistant farm director Ralph Snyder told Jamestown Furniture board members when the Jamestown Tigers finished the season with 47 wins and 75 losses.

"We're shocked over you being shocked!" Haines yelled back.

The Tigers had underestimated the NY-P League, Snyder explained. Their executives still thought in Class D terms instead of what had become a more competitive league as a result of the recent reclassification of the minors.

Haines' difficult job of promoting local baseball had been made nearly impossible by the poor team on the field and he would again have to cover a share of Jamestown Furniture's debt. He wanted no excuses from Detroit and made his feelings clear.

"We like Jamestown and want to continue here," Snyder concluded. "But if there is so much ill feeling over the 1965 season that Detroit could further the cause of baseball here by pulling out, then perhaps that would be the best move."

Haines countered, "Jamestown will have no trouble latching onto a working agreement," and the conversation was over.

E I G H T

$\mathscr{H}$AINES WAS CORRECT. JAMESTOWN HAD NO trouble finding a new major-league affiliation. In October of 1965, the Los Angeles Dodgers won the World Series. One month later, an executive from the Dodgers contacted NY-P League President Vince McNamara to express an interest in fielding a team in the league. McNamara referred the Dodgers to Jamestown and Russ Diethrick negotiated a new working agreement—the same, in principal, to the one Jamestown Furniture City Baseball previously had with the Tigers.

On the field, the Jamestown Dodgers were a disciplined club managed by 26-year-old Bill Berrier, described by Hyde as a "hard-nosed character to whom curfew is as sacred as an Easter Sunrise." Berrier agreed with Hyde's assessment. "When I tell my players to be in at a certain time I don't mean five minutes late."

The 1966 summer was the second year in which the NY-P League used a split season, in which the winners of each half face-off in the playoffs. The Dodgers finished fourth in the first half, then won 10 of their last 11 games to clinch second place for the second half of the season. The story of 1966 was, however, the race for the league batting title between Jamestown Dodgers' right fielder Dave McCammon and Batavia center fielder Cito Gaston.

McCammon was a 20-year-old construction worker from Dade County, Florida with a quick temper. Gaston would go on to spend 11 years in the majors with the Atlanta Braves and San Diego Padres. In 1989, Gaston's first year as manager of the Toronto Blue Jays, he led his club to the American League Championship Series.

McCammon and Gaston were locked in a race for the highest average throughout July and August. With four games to go, both were hitting .332. To heighten the drama, the final four games of the season were all scheduled to be played between Gaston's Trojans and McCammon's Dodgers at College Stadium. The series began with a doubleheader in which Gaston went 4-8 and McCammon went 2-6. Gaston increased his average to .336 and McCammon held even at .332.

"Dodgers vs. Batavia Tonight—But Big Show Is McCammon vs. Gaston," read a large-type headline in Hyde's *Post-Journal* sports section before the third game of the series. McCammon went 2-5 and Gaston was stopped cold with an 0-3 night. Gaston held just a one percentage point lead, .334 to .333.

On the final night of the season, Gaston stepped to the plate in the second inning and singled sharply through the infield. McCammon came up in the bottom of the inning and popped a Texas leaguer over the second base bag. Gaston, in center field, misjudged it and the ball dropped in for a single. The two outfielders were virtually dead-locked for the title.

Gaston struck out his next two at-bats while McCammon drove a double to the outfield wall in the fifth inning and grounded out in the seventh. With the game tied at five, Gaston grounded out in his fourth at-bat in the top of the ninth. McCammon came up in the bottom of the ninth with two outs and the go-ahead run on second base for what would be his final at-bat with the Jamestown Dodgers. "A hit here does it for McCammon," determined Hyde in the press box.

Gaston watched from center field as McCammon topped a ball to the right side of the infield. The Batavia second baseman scrambled back from the second base bag where he had been playing the right-handed McCammon to pull the ball. He raced the bouncing ball to the outfield grass while the Dodgers' winning run rounded third base on his way to home plate. McCammon dug out every step to first base. The ball stopped dead in the thick right field grass as McCammon touched first and, a moment later, the winning run crossed home plate. Gaston stood in center field, stunned, and the batting title was McCammon's, .335 to .333.

A few weeks later, the Dodgers left Jamestown. Dodgers' management, which incurred a $4,000 debt as a result of their season at College Stadium, claimed they always saw Jamestown as an interim operation. "You have everything a baseball fan could wish for except fans and it is a mystery to me," concluded Dodgers Vice President Fresco Thompson.

With the Dodgers gone, Russ Diethrick (who had taken on most of the management duties of Jamestown Furniture since Marty Haines' frustrating season as general manager in 1965) was contacted by the president of the Atlanta Braves. The Braves needed a new Class A affiliation and a working agreement between Jamestown Furniture and Atlanta management was quickly arranged. The arrival of the Braves in the spring of 1967, for some of Jamestown's oldest baseball fans, rekindled memories of the time the Boston Braves played an exhibition game against the Jamestown Spiders at Celoron Park in 1930.

The Spiders were organized soon after the collapse of Billy Webb's 1915 Jamestown Rabbits. Webb wanted to remain in his adopted town and continue to play baseball, so he founded the Spiders to play local semi-pro teams. In 1927, Jake Pitler played against the Spiders with his semi-pro Oil City team. (That same week, Jamestown resident Lucille Ball and the other finalists of a "Miss Jamestown" contest captured the headlines of the Celoron Park newsletter, posing with Miss America of 1927, Beverly Boob.)

The Spiders were composed of a mixture of young players hoping to be discovered and veterans finishing their careers. When the Braves came to play, pitchers Eric "Swat" Erickson and Hugh Bedient were with the Spiders, as was shortstop Vince McNamara, who would one day serve as PONY and NY-P League president.

Erickson, 35 years old and eight years removed from his last major-league game, started against the Braves. "Every [Boston Braves] uniform appeared neat and clean and the athletes looked like tan gods with flashing white teeth," a fan would later recall. Major-league leaders Wally Berger, Hank Gowdy, and George Sisler were among those admired by wide-eyed Jamestowners who filled Celoron Park. Erickson, however, wasn't star-struck and retired the Braves in order over the first two innings. In the bottom of the second, the Spiders loaded the bases and Erickson laced a double to clear the bases.

The score remained 3-0 in favor of the Spiders entering the ninth inning and, more astonishing, Erickson had still not allowed the Boston Braves a hit. Erickson retired the first batter, then pinch hitter Lancelot Richbourg—who had been given the day off and was lounging in his hotel room in Jamestown a half hour earlier—was sent in to bat by Braves manager Bill McKechnie.

Richbourg tapped the first pitch for a "seeing-eye" base hit between first and second and the crowd groaned. Erickson's no-hitter was gone. The next batter reached on an error, but Erickson came back and recorded the final two outs by striking out George Sisler and forcing Wally Berger to fly out to deep center. The man who had begun in Jamestown and rose to the majors with the help of a lemon came home for his brightest moment in baseball, a shutout of the Boston Braves at Celoron Park.

The Braves came to Jamestown in 1967, in part, because the president of the Atlanta Braves organization was John McHale. In 1945, McHale was the first baseman for the World Champion Detroit Tigers and a teammate of future Jamestown Falcons' catcher Russ Kerns. In 1949, McHale and John Jachym were hired to "troubleshoot" for Detroit, a job which required them to meet Marv Olson's Falcons at spring training in Hershey, Pennsylvania. In 1954, McHale was promoted to farm director of the Tigers and convinced management that all Jamestown's operation needed was a good salesman, despite plummeting attendance figures at Municipal Stadium. Hillman Lyons was hired as general manager and the 1954 Falcons doubled their attendance. Also in 1954, McHale fired Danny Litwhiler and replaced him with fiery Wayne Blackburn, who brought the Falcons back from the dead and into the Governors Cup finals. By 1967, McHale already had 20 years of experience with Jamestown baseball.

As president of the Braves, McHale took a liking to a former Chicago Cubs' back-up catcher named Jim Fanning and appointed him Director of Minor League Operations. McHale suggested to Fanning that they consider fielding a team in Jamestown. Fanning contacted Diethrick and the two began a long working relationship. Jamestown Furniture's board members signed the dotted line of another working agreement and Jamestown had a new team, the Jamestown Braves.

The NY-P League was also making changes during the off-season prior to the 1967 season. League President Vince McNamara assembled the NY-P's directors to discuss starting the season in the second week of June, shortening the schedule from 120 to 78 games. The response was favorable. Cold weather had caused major scheduling problems in recent years and players drafted from college would no longer be forced to join their NY-P League teams two months into the season.

Before the 1967 "short season" began, minor-league troubleshooter Warren LaTarte made another visit to put his stamp of approval on the season. "You should do well," he said to Jamestown Braves' representatives. "The Braves have a fine farm system and they will no doubt put some good talent in Jamestown. You also have the advantage of the warm-weather start, which it should have been realized years ago is very important this far north." Closing his briefcase and adjusting his tie, he finished by saying, "I think your club will win the NY-P pennant."

The Jamestown Braves didn't win the pennant but did play .500 baseball, the high point of their season coming in mid-August when they staged a fantastic comeback. With the Braves down 7-0 in the ninth inning, three singles, two wild pitches, three walks, a hit batsman, and a passed ball preceded a three-run homer to give the Braves an 8-7 victory.

The Braves finished in fourth place and per game attendance held steady at roughly 500 a game. Despite McHale and Fanning's efforts, Braves' ownership decided to move all of their minor-league clubs closer to Atlanta for financial reasons. "We do not want to see a city with an excellent park like this one left without baseball," said Fanning. In a well-intentioned gesture, Fanning and McHale obtained assurance from the Houston Astros that they would shift their Class A operation to Jamestown for the 1968 season while the Braves moved their Jamestown operation to Anderson, South Carolina.

The Astros plans changed but the Boston Red Sox' Class A team needed a place to play. Diethrick and Jamestown Furniture were happy to provide College Stadium. In 1968, the Red Sox became the third team in three years to come to Jamestown, and called the new club the Jamestown Falcons.

Red Sox management took "player development" to a whole new level and Diethrick watched in bewilderment as a parade of more than 40 players marched into College Stadium. They were the 1968 Falcons, an example of the Red Sox' approach to the minor leagues in the late 1960s: throw a boat-load of players on the field and see who sticks.

Between 1968 and 1970, the three years during which the Red Sox operated at College Stadium, two field managers shuffled lineups and rosters in Jamestown. Ex-Tigers' catcher Jackie Moore was manager in 1968 and 1969. With thick eyebrows and handsome features, Moore looked like he belonged on the Red Sox. He was tough on the field and affable off the field. Eventually, Moore would manage the Oakland A's from 1984 to 1986 and win the 1990 World Series with Cincinnati.

"You could only put 25 players on your roster each day," Moore remembered years later. "On your line-up card you had to list the 25 you were going to play. Now we had about 45 players and so it was quite a chore to take all your players and put them in uniform and switch them back and forth. A lot of players would come and work out and then go sit in the stands and check the lineup the next day to see if they made the roster or not."

The Falcons' 1970 manager was Jackie Jensen, a former All-American football player with the California Golden Bears who played in the Rose Bowl. In baseball, he hit .279 lifetime in 11 seasons as an outfielder, including an appearance in the 1950 World Series with the Yankees. He went on the voluntary retired list in 1960 because he hated traveling by air. "I still do not like to travel by plane," he told Hyde in 1970. "There were some other factors involved in my decision to retire, but dislike for air travel was the real one." Jensen temporarily overcame his fear of flying and returned to the majors with the Red Sox in 1961 for one final season in the outfield.

Moore and Jensen managed so many players, and rosters were changed so often, that fans had little time to grow attached to their players. Only in retrospect would Jamestowners realize that they had seen special players. First baseman Cecil Cooper was 18 years old in 1968 and would go on to a 17-year career in the majors, hitting a lifetime .298 average. Outfielder Dwight Evans, from Santa Monica, California, would play for the Boston Red Sox throughout the 1970s and 1980s. Ben Oglivie, from Colon, Panama would be a three-time All-Star with the Milwaukee Brewers and spend 16 years in the majors, including a 41 home run season in 1980.

Jamestown did not support the Falcons during the Red Sox' stay at College Stadium. Whether the lack of support was a result of the ever-changing lineups, poor performance (under the Red Sox, the Falcons never finished higher than fifth place), or a simple lack of interest in minor-league baseball, remains debatable. But just 13,049 Jamestowners showed up in 1969, as compared with a high of 143,016 in 1942. Overall, NY-P League attendance suffered as well. Just 168,339 fans came out to NY-P League parks in 1968, compared to 602,273 in 1949.

A rule change was also brought into the NY-P League during the Red Sox' three-year stay in Jamestown. At the end of the 1968 season, Vince McNamara—league president and a member of Major League Baseball's Rules Committee—was asked to try out an experimental "declared pinch-hitter" in the NY-P League. The goal was to make the game more exciting for offense-minded fans. "A hitting specialist," the experimental rule read, "may be designated by the manager prior to the game and included in the line-up card. . . The designated hitting specialist may be used to bat for anyone in the lineup." In 1969, the NY-P League became the first in organized baseball to employ the designated hitter rule, adopted by the American League in 1973.

The 1970 season was notable for the highest number of promotional events since the days when Hillman Lyons was general manager. Diethrick and Jamestown Furniture were willing to try anything to generate interest at College Stadium, so more money was spent on promotions and marketing. Max Patkin, the "Clown Prince of Baseball," came to town. "Little League Night," "PONY Night," and other promotions were also held at College Stadium. As a result, attendance nearly doubled from 1969's all-time low. But when the season was over, Diethrick and his Jamestown Furniture partners gathered over the books to prove what they had feared all along; while attendance rose significantly, costs soared at a greater rate than revenue due to the expense of promotional nights.

At the end of the 1970 season, Diethrick wrote a larger check than usual to help clear Jamestown Furniture's debt. Soon after, the Red Sox front office informed Diethrick and Jamestown Furniture that they would not be returning in 1971 due to the poor condition of College Stadium's facilities.

Professional baseball in Jamestown might not have returned in 1971 if it were not for the Montreal Expos, an expansion team in need of a ballpark. In 1971, as fate would have it, John McHale was president of the Expos and Jim Fanning was their general manager, both having since moved from the Atlanta Braves' front office to Montreal. Fanning and Diethrick agreed upon a new working agreement, then Diethrick helped raise $50,000 in city funds. The Expos also gave the College Stadium grandstand a fresh coat of paint, renovated dugouts, and added a new press box.

In 1971, Fanning promised not to send too many players to College Stadium. He didn't, but the Falcons—under the leadership of field manager and former major-league catcher Eddie Sadowski—were horrible. The 1971 Falcons finished in last place, losing 44 games and winning just 25.

The Jamestown Falcons of 1972, also affiliated with the Expos, were fortunate to have a young manager named Walt Hriniak. By coincidence, Hriniak's mentor was Charlie Lau, a friend of Flo White's, and a former Falcons catcher. Using some of the methods that would later appear in his book, *The Art of Hitting .300*, Lau transformed Hriniak in Class AA from a .250 hitter to a .313 hitter.

Hriniak was called to the majors in 1968 with McHale

and Fanning's Braves. In his first game, Hriniak had two hits off of Juan Marichal and, after the game, Lau was the first person he called. "He had something I'd never seen before in anybody in professional baseball," Hriniak would later say of Lau. "He had tremendous want and need to help people. He was a natural teacher." Hriniak hit just .253 during two seasons in the majors, but under Lau's tutelage he had become a student of the game. After he retired as a player, McHale and Fanning offered Hriniak the managing job in Jamestown, where his mentor had begun his career 20 years earlier.

Larry Parrish was one of Hriniak's players during the 1972 season. Parrish, who would one day play an integral part in the fortunes of professional baseball in Jamestown, would spend 17 years in the majors at third, outfield, and designated hitter. Don Hopkins, Montreal's number one draft pick in 1972 and called "the fastest man in professional baseball" by a Montreal scout, was another. Hopkins would make it to the majors with the Oakland A's in 1975, used primarily as a pinch runner. Even with Parrish and Hopkins in Jamestown, the Falcons were not strong enough to compete with Niagara Falls for the pennant.

For the 1973 season, Fanning again sent Hriniak's Falcons the number one draft pick, Gary Roenicke. Roenicke would spend 12 years in the majors and play in two World Series with Baltimore in 1979 and 1983. He helped keep the Falcons in a tight pennant race eventually lost to Auburn in late August. The Falcons finished at 41-28 but fell short again in their bid for a league championship.

Worst of all, no one seemed to care. After Diethrick's promotion-boosted 1970 season of 25,260 fans, attendance dropped again in 1971 to 12,940. The 1972 and 1973 seasons saw modest increases, but Diethrick and Jamestown Furniture simply couldn't continue to bail out the organization each off-season as they had done for the past 10 years.

"It became apparent Jamestown would no longer support a professional baseball team with sufficient interest to produce a break-even operation," Hyde wrote in September of 1973. "Their efforts and their money were in vain." It was all over for Diethrick and his group, who were as much as $48,000 in debt. Fanning and McHale were notified that there would be no ballclub in Jamestown for the Expos in 1974.

Frank Hyde and Russ Diethrick followed the major leagues from afar during 1974, 1975, and 1976. Gary Roenicke and Larry Parrish made it to the majors with the Expos. Pat Dobson was with the Yankees and then the Indians. John Hiller was with Detroit. In the 1975 playoffs, four former Jamestown players appeared: Jim Rooker and his Pirates lost three straight games to the Reds while, in the American League, Cecil Cooper and Dwight Evans led the Red Sox to three in a row over the Oakland A's and their speedster, Don Hopkins. Ben Oglivie, who played with Evans and Cooper on the 1972 Red Sox, was with Detroit from 1974 to 1977 and would soon join Cooper again in Milwaukee. Greg Mulleavy was still a Dodgers scout and Charlie Lau was the batting coach in Kansas City.

Although there was no Jamestown club in 1974, there was a NY-P League. That was largely due to the efforts of League President Vince McNamara. McNamara was a tough kid from Buffalo. "I had to fight to cross the tracks and serve mass," he would say. "If I hadn't been able to fight back and hold my end up, I would've been stuck in the ground and stepped on." McNamara became the league's president in 1948, a position he would hold for 37 years. But even in 1948, he was no stranger to the PONY League or to Jamestown baseball.

McNamara first came to Jamestown to play ball for Billy Webb's Spiders in the 1920s and was at shortstop for "Swat" Erickson's shutout of the Boston Braves in 1930. In 1939, the first year of PONY League play, McNamara was umpire-in-chief of the league and called Baby Bucs games at Celoron Park. The next year, he called the Falcons' first game—the mid-season inaugural at Allen Park. "Hell, this is more than they drew up there all season," he said at Allen Park that afternoon, comparing the attendance for the opener to the 1939 crowds in Celoron. McNamara was also at "Jamestown Sports Hall of Fame Night" in June of 1957, Jamestown's last NY-P League game until Ernest Kessler and Hillman Lyons revived professional baseball in Jamestown in 1961.

When the Falcons dropped out in 1957, the PONY League was down to six teams and in danger of folding. But during the off-season that followed, McNamara corresponded with the head of the Association of Professional Baseball Leagues. McNamara called for a more favorable allotment of funds to the PONY League and to other leagues in similar situations. By mid-November of 1957, McNamara's efforts resulted in more money to the clubs of his league, making it possible for each team to survive with their current attendance figures. With a more equitable financial arrangement in place, McNamara succeeded in luring two new franchises to the NY-P League and maintaining a semblance of stability during the next three seasons while College Stadium remained dormant. In 1973, McNamara was named the "King of Minor League Baseball" by his peers at the National Association's annual meeting in New Orleans.

But the NY-P League was again down to six teams when Jamestown dropped out before the 1974 season. McNamara would keep the small league alive in 1974, 1975, and 1976. Then, in 1977, the outlook improved for the embattled league. Four teams joined, enough to make two divisions—an East and a West—of five teams each. The new teams were located in Little Falls (Mass.), Utica (N.Y.), Geneva (N.Y.), and Jamestown.

After the 1976 NY-P League season, Russ Diethrick called Jim Fanning of the Expos and asked him to speak with Clefton Farnham, a Jamestown man interested in returning professional baseball to College Stadium. As a boy in Florida, Farnham once caddied for Babe Ruth, Lou Gehrig, and Bill Dickey. (As a tip, Ruth bought Farnham a plane ride with a local pilot for the going rate of one dollar.)

Farnham went on to play baseball and was, oddly enough, a member of Jake Pitler's 1941 Olean Oilers who defeated Greg Mulleavy's Falcons in the Governors Cup finals. Farnham's playing career ended in the Naval Air Force when his plane crashed near Exeter, England, and cracked both his ankles and his wrist.

Fanning met with Farnham and was convinced that a minor-league club could once again be kept afloat in Jamestown. The Montreal Expos took control of the franchise for free and named Farnham general manager of the 1977 Jamestown Expos. Diethrick, recently named Director of Parks and Recreation, was forced to take a less conspicuous role in the operation of the ballclub to avoid any appearance of a conflict of interest. Still, Diethrick served as a liaison between the City of Jamestown and the Montreal Expos and made a stadium rental agreement with Fanning and the Expos.

Part 2
N I N E

"JAMESTOWN TAKES ANOTHER FLING AT PRO
Baseball: Well, here we go again," wrote Frank Hyde prior to
the 1977 season. Hyde could easily be forgiven for his pes-
simism; he had no way of knowing that the new field
manager for the Jamestown Expos, Pat Daugherty, would
soon join Greg Mulleavy and John Newman as the most
engaging personalities ever to wear a Jamestown baseball
uniform.

Daugherty had been in the Expos organization since
1972 and had coached for Hriniak in Jamestown in 1973.
In the off-season, Daugherty was head baseball coach at
Indian Hills Community College in Centerville, Iowa.
During a 15-year career at Indian Hills, his teams won 447
of 596 games, including five state titles. Daugherty was
also elected to the Iowa Coaches Hall of Fame.

He would coach the Jamestown Expos from 1977 to
1981, during which time he drew fans to College Stadium

with his contagious enthusiasm and his team's scrappy style of play. He was Greg Mulleavy and Jake Pitler rolled into one. Known for his umpire-directed tirades on the field, Daugherty compelled Jamestown baseball fans for the first time in decades.

Daugherty also brought a winning attitude to College Stadium. The 1977 season allowed Daugherty a summer to get acquainted with Jamestown and its fans. The Expos finished in second place and attendance was adequate. But it was in 1978 that Daugherty's Expos took root in the community.

Prior to the 1978 season, College Stadium was given a facelift. Jim Fanning, in fact, came from Montreal to help paint while others scrubbed the dugouts and polished the lighting fixtures. Fanning also sent a strong group of ballplayers to College Stadium, including a 6-foot 1-inch first baseman named Anthony Raymond "Razor" Shines. Led by Shines, who would play four years in the majors with Montreal, the 1978 Expos won their first seven games.

Shines demonstrated much of the spirit Daugherty tried to instill in his players. After coming out for a pinch hitter in the eighth inning in an early-season game, Shines stayed involved. "He displayed an all-out effort of cheerleading which had to be an inspiration to his teammates who eventually notched the comeback win," noted the *Post-Journal.* "At 210 pounds, he has to be one of the largest and most persuasive cheerleaders in the area."

The seventh game of the season-opening streak was also the first appearance in Jamestown by infielder Tony Phillips. In the majors, Phillips would lead the American League in walks with 132 in 1993 and runs with 114 in 1992. He would also be a member of the Oakland A's in 1989 when they won the World Series.

The Expos won their eighth straight game 9-3 over Elmira, scoring two off of Bobby Ojeda. Even with the quick start, the Geneva Cubs kept pace. After thirteen games, the Expos and the Cubs were tied with 12-1 records.

The Cubs were becoming the Expos' nemesis and would remain so throughout Daugherty's years as Jamestown's manager.

On July 6, the Expos lost to Geneva 14-8 at College Stadium and the rivalry was officially born—the game had to be delayed 15 minutes to allow a large crowd to click through the turnstiles. Just a little over a year after arriving, Daugherty's teams were packing College Stadium and creating rivalries that hadn't been seen in Jamestown since the hated Olean Oilers came to Municipal Stadium in the early 1940s. The Cubs would continue to get the best of the Expos, beating Jamestown seven out of eight times in 1978.

With one week to go in the 1978 season, the Expos played a wild game against Oneonta at College Stadium that included 20 runs, 23 hits, three home runs, 14 walks, three errors, a balk, and a hit batsman. But most unusual was that Oneonta's starting pitcher had to leave the game when a moth flew into his ear. Expos' trainer Audi Thor rushed to the mound when the pitcher dropped to his knees in the eighth inning. Thor quickly grabbed a pair of tweezers and dislodged the moth by its tail. The Expos won 12-8 but were still stuck in second place, seven games behind Geneva, where they would finish the season.

The Jamestown/Geneva rivalry continued in 1979, with both teams jumping to another fast start. By mid-June, the Expos and Cubs had split a four-game season series and were tied for first place. Then the Expos pitching staff faltered, allowing 53 runs and 78 hits in the next six games to fall behind the steady Cubs.

As quickly as they dropped, however, Daugherty's club snapped back and won eight in a row behind timely hitting and revitalized pitching. Expos pitcher Buddy Maher had a 2-3 record with a 5.46 ERA before the streak. In 10 days, his ERA dropped to 3.51 and his record climbed to 6-3. Jamestown was back in the race, only three games behind Geneva. As in 1978, though, the Cubs were too strong, and took two out of three in a three game series to knock the Expos out of contention.

The 1980 season was no contest. The Expos were horrible on the road, losing 22 of 30 games away from home at one point. By early August, the Cubs sewed up their division. With no pennant race to bring excitement to College Stadium, Daugherty sometimes had to generate interest in other ways.

On August 26, College Stadium was quiet after the Auburn Americans jumped out to a 2-0 lead, Daugherty sensed a lack of energy from his team and from the fans. Before the game, Daugherty's catcher had been entertaining his teammates with his harmonica in the bullpen. So during the seventh inning stretch, Daugherty suggested the catcher hold a concert over the PA system. The crowd quickly came to life and the Expos responded with four runs to win the game. "The noise in the stadium sounded like the two teams were fighting for the pennant instead of second place in the Western Division nearly 20 games behind Geneva," reported the *Post-Journal.* Jamestown won its next two against Auburn to close out the season.

Despite the Expos' poor overall performance in 1980, Daugherty's first four years as manager in Jamestown were impressive on the field and in the stands. His 1977-1980 clubs won 151 and lost 129, with two second-place finishes. The Expos' 44 wins in 1978 were the most for a Jamestown club since the NY-P League went to a short-season schedule in 1967. Daugherty was named NY-P League Manager of the Year twice. Annual attendance at College Stadium rose each of Daugherty's first four years—from 17,938 in 1977 to 48,078 in 1980—while NY-P League attendance remained steady. Their 1980 attendance was the highest since 1962, Hillman Lyons' final year as general manager of the Jamestown Tigers.

The 1980 season was also the summer Frank Hyde retired after nearly 35 years as *Post-Journal* sports editor. "During my 25 years in the newspaper field," said *Post-Journal* Publisher Earl S. Champlin, "I have never met an employee who has shown more dedication to his job than Frank Hyde has the *Post-Journal*. The Jamestown area has been very fortunate to have a sportswriter of his caliber."

Hyde, an Honorary Gold Card Member of the National Association of Baseball League Writers, lifetime honorary member of the neighboring town of Gerry's Fire Department, the Jamestown YMCA, the Chautauqua Lake Yacht Club, and the National Association of Approved Basketball Officials also served for 20 years on the Heisman Award Committee of New York. In 1969, Hyde was given the Service Award by *Sport* magazine. "Through his sensitive, informative writings over the years, Frank Hyde has been an overall affirmative voice in the community in the field of sports," *Sport* reported.

Hyde was honored at College Stadium with a night of his own between games of a doubleheader on August 20, 1980. League President Vince McNamara and Expos' Vice President Jim Fanning, along with other baseball and non-baseball acquaintances, were there to wish him a happy retirement. Hyde was 77 years old when he died three years later, in 1984.

Daugherty's first four years as Jamestown's manager also saw the return of Flo White, since married and known as Flo Wick. Since she won season tickets in a 1951 raffle, Flo had three children and saw her mother ("Mom" to the ballplayers of the 1950s) pass away. Unable to take her babies to the park every night, Flo attended ballgames only sporadically during the 1960s and early 1970s. But when the Expos returned in 1977, so did Flo and her goat bell. She immediately became a huge Pat Daugherty fan.

Flo became "Mom" to a new generation of ballplayers in Jamestown. In 1978, Flo also did her best to help bring the Expos good luck. Daugherty's coach was Nick Testa, a former coach and catcher for the San Francisco Giants. Testa's mother, 81-year-old Frances Testa, accompanied her son to Jamestown for the summer. Prior to every home and away game, "Mama" Testa stood out in front of the

Expos' dugout to sprinkle Holy Water on the ballplayers. As the season progressed, Razor Shines and his teammates would call for the Holy Water if Mama Testa was late. In mid-August, she had to leave Jamestown and return to her home in New York City. Before she left, Mama Testa handed Flo a jar of the Holy Water and asked her to continue the ritual for the last two weeks of the season. Flo did her duty and the Expos finished in second place with their best record since 1954.

In 1981, Daugherty's new team of Jamestown Expos arrived with a 17-year-old rookie from Venezuela named Andres Galarraga. "Unfortunately he couldn't speak English," recalled Flo. "The only words he could say were 'Hamburg' and 'Coke.'"

"We went on a road trip to Geneva that summer and the motel we stayed at was the same one the players stayed at," Flo recalled. "We were right across the street from a McDonald's. We saw him walking back after the game and the kids went up to him and started talking and throwing the Frisbee. Before they knew it, it was midnight. He was just enjoying being with the kids and they loved him to pieces. It was like that for the whole four days of the road trip."

Galarraga hit six home runs and batted .261 in Jamestown in 1981. "The Big Cat" made it to the majors with Montreal from 1985 to 1991, then St. Louis in 1992. Also an All-Star first baseman, Galarraga led the majors in hitting with a .370 batting average in 1993 on the expansion Colorado Rockies.

As Galarraga moved up in organized baseball, Flo and her children followed his career. "Look, there's Andres!" the kids would say when they saw him on TV. "We're going to be watching you," Flo would tell players when they left Jamestown. "If we can help push you there, we'll push."

With the major-league players on strike, the first week of the 1981 season was marked by an unusual stoppage of play in a game against the Sailors in Erie, Pennsylvania. The Sailors' pitcher was working on a no-hitter in the fifth inning

Jim Leyland, long-time manager of the Pittsburgh Pirates, as catcher for the
1965 Jamestown Tigers.

Dave McCammon (#7) during the 1966 season, in the midst of a batting race with Cito Gaston.

Clockwise, starting with (top-left) Pat Daugherty, Gene Glynn, Dan Lunetta, and Frank Wren. Each played important roles in the survival of minor league baseball in Jamestown during the late 1970s and the 1980s. Daugherty and Glynn eventually took jobs with the expansion Colorado Rockies, while Lunetta and Wren took jobs with the expansion Florida Marlins.

Q. V. Lowe, whose tremendous achievements as Jamestown Expos pitching coach were overshadowed by tragedy in 1992.

Together, Russ "Mr. Baseball" Diethrick and Greg Peterson saved minor league baseball in Jamestown during a tense week in October of 1993.

Marquis Grissom, Jamestown Expos' outfielder in 1988, signing an
autograph at College Stadium.

The 1989 Expos win Jamestown's first championship in 56 years.

The first pitch in Florida Marlins' history, at Ainsworth Field in Erie, Pennsylvania, against the Expos.

when the game was abruptly halted. The base umpire had to leave the game because his wife was having labor pains in the stands. The home plate umpire asked Mark Schumacher, a Class AA umpire from Erie who happened to be at the game, to fill in. When the game resumed, the next Expos' batter hit a long single off the right field wall to break up the no-hitter. That was the only hit the Expos managed against the Sailors and Daugherty's club lost 7-0.

The game in Erie was one of only two losses for the Expos in their first eight games of 1981. However, with Daugherty's club going into a three-game series in Geneva, the Cubs were again in first place with only one loss. Geneva took the first game and it appeared that Jamestown would once again look up at Geneva in the standings throughout the season. But Daugherty's club took the next two games and the Expos won their first series in Geneva sin e Pat Daugherty became Jamestown's manager. Daugherty, who would be named NY-P Manager of the Year again in 1981, never allowed his Expos to falter.

"Ten years of professional baseball and I never won it," said an elated Daugherty after clinching the Western Division in the final week of August. "I finished second a lot of times." The joy did not last long, though, because Daugherty had to return to his teaching and coaching duties at Indian Hills Community College. The school's administration would not allow him to arrive late for the semester; hitting coach Frank Wren would manage the team in Daugherty's absence. Daugherty said his good-byes and flew back to Iowa with three games still to play in the regular season and was not expected to return for the playoffs.

Frank Wren was a second baseman and outfielder for Daugherty's Expos in 1978. He was Jamestown's Most Valuable Player that season with a .320 batting average, perhaps given a boost by Mama Testa's pre-game Holy Water blessings. Wren advanced to the Expos' West Palm Beach club of the Florida State League where he played in 1979 and 1980. On the fifth day of spring training in 1981, Wren began having neck spasms followed by headaches and nausea. Tests determined that he had a brain tumor attached to a cranial nerve just above the back of his neck. The tumor was benign, but it was still in a crucial area that effects speech and swallowing. Surgery to remove the tumor was successful and in nine days Wren was up and walking again. But three weeks later, he was still experiencing double vision and weakness which prevented him from taking even a brisk walk.

While still recovering, Wren received a call from the Expos' Jim Fanning, who offered him the Jamestown coaching job. "I'll go in a minute," Wren said. "I loved playing for [Daugherty]."

At the end of the 1981 season, Daugherty was in Iowa and Wren was in charge of the Expos as they prepared for the most highly anticipated baseball series in Jamestown in almost 30 years. Wren's Expos were set for the 1981 finals against the Oneonta Yankees, a team which won their division every year from 1977 to 1981 with an average victory margin of eight-and-a-half games. Three of these years the Yankees won the league championship.

Just hours before the start of the first game, Daugherty surprised everyone in the NY-P League by showing up in Oneonta to manage his team. Daugherty convinced his superiors at Indian Hills Community College to allow him to fly back to the Expos and Wren gladly returned to being his coach.

Unfortunately, even Daugherty's arrival couldn't help the Expos in game one, a 7-1 loss. For the second game of the series, at College Stadium, future major-league pitcher Bob Tewksbury started for Oneonta. The Expos scored three in the bottom of the seventh off of Tewksbury. Then Jamestown pitcher Randy St. Claire, who would appear in a World Series with the Atlanta Braves in 1991, got the win in relief by allowing just one hit in three innings. The Expos won 8-5 to even up the best-of-three series at one game apiece. One game was left to determine the 1981 NY-P League champion.

The Yankees scored six in the first two innings and took an 8-1 lead into the bottom of the ninth. The Expos came up to bat for their final three outs. In the bottom of the ninth, the first two Expos reached base safely, then Oneonta's reliever came back with two quick outs. A three run home run made the score 8-4. Another homer made it 8-5. A single, followed by a Galarraga double off the top of the fence put men on second and third with two outs and brought the tying run to the plate. But the miracle comeback fell short as the final batter flied out to strand both runners and close out the 1981 season and Pat Daugherty's run as manager of the Jamestown Expos. During the off-season, Daugherty was promoted by the Expos and continued his climb in professional baseball.

Jamestown fans were once again supporting their baseball team, and Russ Diethrick was looking ahead. Like Kessler and Judge Bargar before him, Diethrick knew the importance of a ballpark. He also saw that College Stadium was slowly crumbling. Diethrick knew that without a suitable ballpark, Jamestown would eventually lose their team to a city that had a better facility. Major-league clubs needed structurally sound ballparks to develop their high-priced talent and College Stadium was no longer considered one of the premiere places to play in Class A baseball.

A study to determine the cost of renovating College Stadium was authorized by Diethrick. It revealed that "immediate action must be taken or irreversible damage will occur to the roof, steel, and concrete." It also suggested that new seats should be installed and interior finishes, utilities, and security be added to the press box.

Between 1982 and 1984, stadium renovation plans were made and Jamestowners continued to support their team despite uninspired play by the Expos. In each of the three seasons, Dan Lunetta was general manager and Milbry E. "Moby" Benedict was field manager. Lunetta went to

Jamestown High School and Jamestown Community College. In 1979, Diethrick helped get him a job as a College Stadium groundskeeper. In 1980 and 1981, Lunetta served as public relations director before being promoted to general manager in 1982.

Benedict was a shortstop at the University of Michigan and, following graduation, played in the Detroit minor-league system. In 1959, he returned to his Alma Mater as an assistant coach to Don Lund (the Detroit Tigers' farm director who incorrectly predicted that Jamestown's club would win the NY-P League in 1965). Benedict took over Lund's job in 1963 and remained head coach for 17 years at Michigan.

In 1982 and 1983, Benedict's Expos finished second in their division with a combined 76-76 record. The 1984 season saw the Expos field the worst team in the NY-P League, a club with no All-Stars and no .300 hitters. On August 30, the Expos lost their ninth straight. "Most people do not prefer rain on Labor Day," wrote *Post-Journal* sports editor Jim Riggs, "but the Jamestown Expos were happy to see the precipitation because it canceled their final NY-P League game."

In 1983, the NY-P League's most notable team was the Utica Blue Sox, an independent club made famous by Roger Kahn's *Good Enough to Dream*. The Blue Sox would go on to win the Eastern Division in a furious race and win two out of three games in the post-season to cap their Cinderella season. Jamestown fell twice to the Blue Sox, including a game in which Utica pitcher Mike Zamba allowed only one Jamestown run despite giving up 12 hits.

Though the mediocrity of the 1982, 1983, and 1984 seasons was frustrating for Jamestown baseball fans, the action on the field was secondary to the construction around it. By 1984, Diethrick had secured close to $500,000 for stadium renovations. In 1984, College Stadium received two public rest rooms, two new locker rooms, a changing room with toilet and shower for game officials, a stadium operations office with secretarial and waiting space, a first aid room, a groundskeepers' storage area, a concession stand with enclosed storage, and a new grandstand roof. In 1985, the grandstand was refurbished, new dugouts were constructed, the sound system was redone, and a new press box was added. Also, a new electronic scoreboard was placed in left field.

As a result of the renovation, Diethrick was able to attract the Babe Ruth World Series for 16- to 18-year-olds to Jamestown, where it would continue to be hosted for more than 10 years.

Jamestowners could once again argue that their ballpark was the finest in the NY-P League. Thanks largely to Diethrick's commitment, minor-league baseball's future appeared bright at College Stadium.

T E N

VINCE MCNAMARA RETIRED AS NY-P LEAGUE PRESident in 1985 after 37 years of service. McNamara's replacement was former *Auburn Citizen* sports editor Leo Pinckney, who inherited a strong 12-team league which had topped the 500,000 mark in attendance in 1983 for the first time since the late 1940s.

In Jamestown, Frank Wren returned to College Stadium, this time as general manager, after coaching in the Montreal minor-league system in 1982 and 1983. The 1985 Falcons' field manager was Ed Creech, called "a throwback to the days of Pat Daugherty," according to *Post-Journal* sports editor Jim Riggs, with regards to his "aggressive style of managing and his energetic personality."

Creech's pitching staff included 22-year-old Randy Johnson, a 6-foot 10-inch future All-Star who would strike out 308 batters in 1993 to lead the American League. The tallest pitcher in major-league history, Johnson was considered a strong prospect in 1985 because of his overpowering fastball, but his temper was already a problem. "One concern is Johnson's ability to handle frustration," read a scouting report. "He missed a month last season because he broke his right hand slugging a dugout wall."

The Expos edged the Erie Cardinals and the Niagara Falls Rapids to win their division with a 45-33 record and Expos fans were again hoping for their first championship in over 30 years. As part of a new playoff system, the Expos would face the Auburn Astros, winners of the Central Division, in a one-game playoff. The winner of the one-game semi-final round would advance to a best-of-three championship series.

The Expos struck out 15 times and managed just three hits to lose 6-0. After being ousted from the playoffs at Auburn's dilapidated Falcon Park, Creech and his Expos were forced to wait for two hours because their bus wouldn't start. "This about sums up the night," said Jamestown's losing pitcher.

Wren was named Montreal's assistant scouting director that off-season. Upon his recommendation, he was replaced by Tom Prohaska, a former Jamestown Community College baseball coach. Field manager Creech was replaced by former Jamestown Expos' player Gene Glynn. For Daugherty's 1979 Expos, Glynn had hit .348 and led the league in both runs scored and stolen base percentage. Since leaving Jamestown, he played and coached in the Expos organization.

Glynn's 1986 and 1987 Jamestown Expos distinguished themselves as terrible fielders, but were also flush with future major-leaguers. While the second-place 1987 team fared significantly better than the last-place 1986 club, both were plagued by costly mistakes.

On June 21, 1986, a throwing error and a bloop to center, in which three Expos converged on a ball that dropped for a single, gave Jamestown a ninth-inning loss to Geneva. On July 8, 1986 the Expos committed six errors in a loss to Auburn. Two nights later, Glynn's Expos made three errors in one inning to give up seven unearned runs as the Oneonta Yankees—with their catcher Jim Leyritz and their second baseman Andy Stankiewicz—won 8-3. The Expos committed 19 errors in 10 games during one notable stretch in 1986. On opening day in 1987, three costly errors—all by Expos pitchers—led to three unearned Erie runs and helped give the Cardinals a 7-3 victory. "Batavia Outlasts Jamestown In Comedy Of Errors," read the *Post-Journal* headline on August 5, 1987, as Jamestown players committed six more errors (two by second baseman Delino DeShields) in a 6-5 loss to the Trojans.

DeShields was the quintessential player on Glynn's Expos— a top prospect who couldn't field. In 33 games, 18-year-old DeShields made 24 errors. "I remember not being able to catch a ground ball," said DeShields in 1993 as a member of the Montreal Expos. "A lot of frustrating moments in that league."

Mike Blowers, John Vanderwal, and Archi Cianfrocco all played for Glynn in Jamestown. Blowers was a right-handed third baseman born in Wurzburg, Germany who made it to the majors in 1989 with the Yankees. Vanderwal, who hit .500 in 50 at-bats during his short time in Jamestown, made it to Montreal in 1991. Angelo Dominic "Archi" Cianfrocco, a 6-foot 5-inch infielder from Rome, New York, debuted with Montreal in 1992.

In 1988, Glynn was replaced by Roger LaFrancois, a former Red Sox catcher who caught the longest minor-league game of all time, between Rochester (N.Y.) and Pawtucket (R.I.). The Jamestown Expos were again blessed with several top prospects on their way to the majors. Future All-Star Marquis Grissom had a horrible start at the plate in Jamestown. "That was the worst start for me ever," he recalled. "I was close to packin' it up in Jamestown for the first six weeks. Somehow I got started and that's when my career took off." Even with his slow start, Grissom appeared in 74 of Jamestown's 76 games in 1988, and hit .323 with eight homers and 69 runs scored. At 16 years old, shortstop Wilfredo Nieva "Wil" Cordero was the youngest player in organized baseball when he started his professional baseball career in Jamestown. Cordero went on to the majors with the Expos, where he would make the All-Star team and hit .294 in 1994.

Part of the reason for the Expos' success in moving players up to the majors was their coaching staff, in particular pitching coach Q. V. Lowe. In 1972, Lowe was pitching coach for Leo Durocher's Chicago Cubs of Ferguson Jenkins, Milt Pappas, Burt Hooten, Juan Pizarro, and 1956 Jamestown Falcons' right-hander Phil Regan. By coincidence, Lowe was also coach of Oneonta in 1981 when his Yankees overcame the surprise return of Pat Daugherty to beat the Jamestown Expos in the NY-P finals. In 1985, Lowe took the pitching coach position in Jamestown under manager Ed Creech. Lowe returned to Jamestown in 1987, where he would stay for the next seven years.

"This is the most rewarding of all coaching positions," Lowe said of his job in Jamestown. "By the time they get to Double A, the guys kind of stop listening to you and by Triple A you're just a bump on a log. In the big leagues, it's absolutely a farce.

In 1988, Lowe's pitching staff led the NY-P League with a team ERA of 2.68. The Expos' two top starters, Danilo Leon and Dan Freed, combined for a 23-4 record on the season. Leon, a right-hander from LaConcepcion, Venezuela, would pitch for the Texas Rangers in 1992. In 1992, Leon had a 1.16 ERA. Freed finished with a remarkable 0.67 ERA; he allowed just nine earned runs in 121 innings pitched. Lowe was considered such a good coach that, early in 1988, future Hall of Fame pitcher Don Sutton asked Lowe to work with his son, a pitching prospect.

Led by Grissom, and Lowe's pitching staff, the 1988 Expos were in first place on July 29 when the Little Falls Mets came to College Stadium for a memorable game. Freed started and allowed just two runs in nine innings, but the

Expos were held scoreless until a two-run home run tied the game in the bottom of the ninth. Freed retired the Mets in the 10th inning and was taken out for a reliever in the 11th.

The score was still tied with two outs and no one on base in the bottom of the 17th inning, when Grissom came to the plate for the Expos. Grissom hit a line drive to right-center field that Little Falls catcher Todd Hundley would remember six years later; he described the play sitting in the home dugout of Shea Stadium in New York before a game between Grissom's Montreal Expos and Hundley's New York Mets. "I'm thinking double, maybe triple," Hundley said. "So the outfielder gets to the ball and I look up and this guy's around third base." The throw came home but Grissom slid head-first in front of Hundley's tag to complete the game-winning inside-the-park home run. Right-center field at College Stadium, 410 feet deep, was known from that day forward as "Grissom Gardens."

The Expos continued to play well, but the Erie Orioles kept pace and, on August 29, Jamestown's lead was trimmed to just one game. Then, just as in 1981, Jamestown's manager had to return to school. Roger LaFrancois, a physical education teacher at Killingly High School in Connecticut, was given no option to stay in Jamestown by the school's superintendent. This time, there would be no reprieve like the one Daugherty received. So after losing two days pay from Killingly, LaFrancois left the Expos in the hands of Lowe and batting coach Kevin Malone. The next night, the Expos split a doubleheader with Batavia while Erie won their game to cut the Jamestown lead to a half-game going into the final night of the season.

The two teams were set to play one game at Erie's Ainsworth Field to decide which team would win the division and go on to the playoffs. Freed took a 1-0 lead into the bottom of the ninth before giving up a game-tying, lead-off home run. The Expos scored again in the top of the 10th on two Erie errors. In the bottom of the 10th, the Orioles made their final out on a close play at the plate. The Expos won the game 2-1 and clinched the 1988 division title.

But Jamestown's club would again fall short of winning the league championship (now called the McNamara Cup, in honor of the former NY-P League President) for the 29th consecutive season. The 1989 Expos lost to Oneonta, led by their second baseman, Pat Kelley, who went 6 for 11 in the two games. After a rain-out in Oneonta, the Expos lost 2-1 and dropped the next game, in Jamestown, 5-3 in 13 innings to close out the best-of-three series despite Grissom's 5 for 11 hitting performance. Roger LaFrancois, still in Connecticut, was named 1988 NY-P League Manager of the Year.

LaFrancois did not return for the 1989 season. His replacement was Don Werner, who had caught Tom Seaver's only no-hitter in 1978 as Johnny Bench's back-up for the Cincinnati Reds. The 1989 season also brought a new general manager, Tom O'Reilly. O'Reilly left his job at an Illinois office supply company in order to come to Jamestown. He replaced Tom Prohaska, who was not offered a new contract by Montreal.

For the second year in a row, the Expos won their division on the last night of the season. Werner's team was tied with Niagara Falls before the Expos crushed Erie 15-1 and Niagara Falls lost an extra-innings heart-breaker to Welland (Ontario) to put Jamestown in the NY-P League finals against the Pittsfield (Mass.) Mets.

The Mets finished with the best record in the NY-P league in 1989. Led by future major-leaguers Curtis Pride, Tito Navarro, Patrick Howell, and Dave Telgheder, the Mets beat the Expos three out of four times during the regular season. Werner's Expos were thin in top prospects, but had a knack for winning come-from-behind ballgames. In 1989, the Jamestown Expos won 14 games in the eighth, ninth, and 10th innings.

And that's what they did in game one of the best-of-three series which began in Jamestown. The Mets took a 3-1 lead into the bottom of the ninth. With just three outs to work with against a Mets' closer who saved 18 games that season, the Expos hit three consecutive singles, then a triple off the right field fence to win the opener 4-3. After the game, the Mets chartered a flight back to Pittsfield to rest for game two, scheduled for the next night. The Expos, meanwhile, traveled eight hours by bus across New York State and into Western Massachusetts. Werner's Jamestown club was flat in game two after the long trip and lost to the Mets 4-2. Still, the Expos remained just one game away from ending Jamestown's championship drought.

The tie-breaker the next night was a tense pitchers' duel. Going into the seventh, the game was still scoreless when Expos' left fielder Derek Hudson hit a soft single and came around to score on a double. Hudson's was the only run of the game, as Lowe's pitching staff held the Mets scoreless and the Expos won the McNamara Cup, Jamestown's first league championship in 36 years.

Shortly before the 1990 season, Montreal management decided to move Werner up to their Class AA team in Jacksonville, Florida. Pat Daugherty, who had been scouting in Florida since 1986, was offered the job; he accepted without hesitation and Jamestown fans like Flo Wick were overjoyed to have him back.

Daugherty's 1990 Expos were a streaky team led by Robbie Katzaroff, a replacement player for the Florida Marlins during the baseball strike of 1994. For the Expos in 1990, he hit .364 to win the league batting title and was named NY-P League Rookie of the Year.

The most memorable night of the season came when Expos' right-hander Bob Baxter took the mound at College Stadium in the second game of a doubleheader. He came to a set position and looked to his catcher, Dan Hargis, for the sign. Baxter shook his head, confused by Hargis' signs, and stepped off the mound.

"Now we have time called," said radio announcer Pete Hubbell, calling the game live on WJTN radio with his partner,

Skip Pierce. "There's some confusion between the pitcher and the catcher. Let's get it together here."

"How can you get messed up on the first pitch of the ballgame?" asked Pierce.

Baxter walked back to the mound and looked to his catcher again but Hargis was wagging his hand back and forth, patting his left knee, and clenching his fist. Baxter was bewildered. The usual signs between Baxter and Hargis were simple: one finger for a fastball, two for a curveball, and three for a slider. Embarrassed and confused, Baxter decided to ignore Hargis' bizarre signs and throw a fastball. In mid-wind-up, the plate umpire called time and charged to the mound, trailed by Hargis.

"What's going on here kid?" yelled the umpire.

"He's not putting down a number," said a shaken Baxter.

Then Hargis: "You know the signals, let's go."

Twice more, Baxter tried to get the signs from Hargis with no luck.

"Maybe it's time for Baxter to get a set of glasses," said Pierce for WJTN. "They ought to take him to the optometrist and get his eyes examined."

Finally, Daugherty charged to the mound. "You've pitched since you were what? In little league?" He patted his pitcher and jogged back to the dugout.

Baxter tried again, but could not get the signs straight from Hargis.

"This is one of the most unbelievable things in the history of professional baseball," said Hubbell from the press box as the home plate umpire walked deliberately to the mound, pointed to Baxter, and threw him out of the ballgame.

As Baxter walked off the mound to the dugout, the umpire took off his mask and put his arm around Baxter's shoulder.

"My name is Peter Funt," he said, "and I do the Candid Camera show." Funt pointed up to the grandstand roof where a hidden camera was recording the prank. "And you are one of the nicest guys we have ever caught on Candid Camera, although you are shaking like a leaf."

Over the PA system, announcer Todd Peterson filled in the confused spectators. "Your attention, please, ladies and gentlemen. We'd like you all to smile because you and the Expos are on Candid Camera." The crowd cheered as the camera panned the bleachers.

"And we've all been taken," added Hubbell for his radio listeners.

"I was sensing this club was willing to go the extra mile," Funt said when asked why he chose Jamestown for the stunt. "I had a warm feeling here."

Baxter returned to the mound that night and retired the first nine batters he faced, four of the first five on strikeouts on his way to a complete game four-hitter over the Rapids. "I wanted to get on TV some way," said Baxter after the game. "This wasn't the way I was planning on doing it."

The Expos finished the 1990 season by winning three in a row, then losing two straight in the playoffs, 14-3 and 5-4, to the Erie Sailors.

The 1991 Expos started the season strong under the same man who managed the Expos in 1985, Ed Creech. Creech's team opened the season with four wins and no losses, prompting him to tell his players that he would shave his head if they won 10 games in a row. Creech's Expos won nine games before finally losing one. "I feel pretty good about keeping my hair," said Creech. "But I don't feel good about the streak coming to an end."

The Expos stayed in first place from opening day to the final day of the season. Another spectacular Lowe-led pitching staff included future major-leaguers Brian Looney and Heath Haynes. Looney, who led the league with a 1.16 ERA and a 7-1 record, would go to the majors with Montreal in 1993. Haynes, the Expos closer, had 10 wins, 11 saves, 93 strikeouts, and a 2.08 ERA. He would make it up to Montreal in 1994.

Derek White, a 6-foot 2-inch, 220 pound first baseman,

was another future Montreal Expos player. Under Creech in Jamestown, White hit .328 with 49 RBIs to lead Jamestown at the plate. The Expos, as a team, would lead the league in hitting with a .266 team average.

By early August, their division lead swelled to over 10 games. Expos mascot Whirlin' the Wizard, played by Jamestowner Gordon Marsh and introduced by general manager Tom O'Reilly, helped keep fans entertained while their team ran away with the division. "Whirlin' has been interested in sporting events ever since his Uncle Merlin took him to his first jousting match in Camelot," read O'Reilly's introduction in the 1991 program. Whirlin' was one of O'Reilly's many business and marketing contributions to Jamestown baseball during his five years with the club, starting in 1989.

Whirlin's only predecessor at College Stadium was "Yippee," a variation of Montreal's mascot "Youpee," played by Jamestowner Jeff Brucculeri. Brucculeri was a PA announcer at College Stadium who made so many mistakes that he was forced to quit. After being ousted, Brucculeri developed the character and pitched Yippee to general manager Dan Lunetta who didn't like the idea, according to sports editor Riggs (who didn't like it either). Brucculeri persisted. He purchased the costume himself—a blue bear with a flat face and an Expos jersey—and badgered Lunetta until he acquiesced. Yippee was an instant success with the kids at College Stadium and Brucculeri was a natural at his job. (Brucculeri later took a job at a Tulsa radio station where he broadcasted Tulsa Oilers Hockey and Oral Roberts University basketball. He went on to become the mascot for the Tulsa Fastbreakers of the Continental Basketball Association, using his Yippee costume with a Fastbreakers jersey to play "Bubby Breaker.")

As in 1990, the 1991 Jamestown Expos faced Erie in a one-game semi-final playoff round to qualify for the finals. With one out in the bottom of the eighth and Erie up 1-0, Expos shortstop Mark Grudzielanek stepped to the plate. A

In 1993, seven ex-Jamestown Expos made the Montreal Expos' Opening Day roster. In the back row (from left to right) Delino DeShields, Wilfredo Cordero, Brian Barnes, and Marquis Grissom. Kneeling (from left to right) are Tim Laker, John VanderWal (1987), and Archi Cianfrocco (1987).

The Jammers beat Batavia in 12 innings to win their division in a one-game playoff in 1994.

future major-league shortstop with Montreal, Grudzielanek fouled an 0-2 pitch off the plate. The ball bounced up and hit him in the eye, forcing him out of the game. Grudzielanek's replacement, who inherited the two-strike count, knocked a rally-starting single. The Expos scored five runs and sent nine men to the plate before the inning was over, to earn an opportunity to play the Pittsfield Mets in a rematch of the 1989 finals.

The Expos won the opener in Pittsfield and returned to College Stadium the next night. Whirlin' stood on the home dugout chanting, "Let's Go Expos," into his white megaphone, to an organ accompaniment, as the Expos blew the game open in the eighth inning with four runs. With each hit, Flo's goat bell rang out, and Jamestown's second league championship in two years drew closer.

Staked to a 4-0 lead, Haynes struck out the first batter in the top of the ninth. College Stadium seemed ready to burst when a walk, an error, and an infield single loaded the bases. Haynes forced the next batter into a sacrifice fly, which scored the Mets' first run of the game and left them with two outs. The next batter grounded out to short and the Jamestown dugout emptied. Creech ran to the mound ahead of his club and catcher Mike Daniel lifted Haynes off his feet. The McNamara Cup was raised by the Expos who celebrated around the pitcher's mound. Jamestown again had the NY-P League's best team.

From the time Daugherty came to Jamestown in 1977 to the close of the 1991 season, College Stadium was home to two championships and five division titles. Expos won three batting titles, two Rookie of the Year awards, and five Manager of the Year awards. Like the 1940s and early 1950s, the period since Daugherty's arrival was unquestionably another "golden age" for Jamestown professional baseball.

The Expos opened the 1992 season in Erie, where six television cameras from Florida's Sunshine Network recorded every move of the first game in Florida Marlin's history. The 1992 Erie Sailors were the first of the Marlins' farm teams to play a game (the major-league expansion club did not begin playing until 1993). Along with the national press, the entire Marlins' front office was on hand, including Director of Minor League Administration Dan Lunetta and Assistant General Manager Frank Wren.

Both expansion clubs—the Marlins and the Colorado Rockies—drew much of their front office talent from the highly regarded Montreal Expos organization. The result was a dizzying web of Jamestown-related baseball connections.

Lunetta and Wren went to Florida. Lunetta, the former College Stadium groundskeeper, continued to work for the Expos for two years before spending time with the Cincinnati Reds and the Buffalo Bisons. Lunetta returned to the Expos as Director of Team Travel before accepting the Marlins' offer. Wren, who coached the Expos when Daugherty was manager and Lunetta was general manager, stayed in the Montreal organization (including a year as general manager of the Jamestown Expos) until the Marlins hired him.

In Colorado, Pat Daugherty was named Director of Scouting and Gene Glynn was given the managing job of Colorado's Class A farm team. Glynn, who played for Jamestown while Lunetta was groundskeeper, was given the job of Coordinator of Instruction for the Rockies. In 1994, Glynn would became Colorado's first-base coach. Other former Jamestown baseball characters with the Rockies included Dwight Evans (batting coach), Pat Dobson (scout), and Jim Fanning (scout).

The Expos, managed by Q. V. Lowe, beat the Sailors in 13 innings that afternoon and seemed to be picking up where they had left off in 1991.

E L E V E N

IN JAMESTOWN DURING THE 1830s, A GAME WAS played with a wooden bat and a ball in which runners were called out only when pegged by a thrown ball. Children played it in the hills outside of town and in an empty lot near the local tannery. The game evolved into "baseball" and Jamestown children started playing it on a swampland called the Flats. The swampland was often covered by row boats and rafts but, when the water level dropped, the land served as an early ballfield. By the late 1850s, the rules of the game were still only roughly defined and the ball they used was rock hard, making it common for teams to score 60 or 70 runs.

Jamestown was little more than a village in the mid-1800s and Celoron was a tiny hamlet still 30 years short of having an amusement park. Boats filled the stream along the five-mile stretch between Chautauqua Lake (at Celoron) and Jamestown. One could look south along the stream from a rickety wooden bridge to see boats carrying logs and lumber on their way over the border to Warren, and then on to Pittsburgh. The hills to the west were full of fine-furniture shops for which Jamestown was already renowned.

On July 4, 1861, thin and athletic Jamestowner Clint Winsor turned 14 years old. The Civil War had begun and boys a few years older than him had already left town to join the battle. While they fought, Winsor sat in the classroom of a one-room schoolhouse near the center of the village.

The war continued and Winsor attended high school at Jamestown Union School and Collegiate Institute where he excelled in sports, particularly gymnastics, which led him to compete against schools in neighboring towns. He and his teammates were a big hit at the New York State Teacher's Association at Owego in 1868 with their demonstration in free, dumbbell, and wand gymnastics.

In 1866, 19-year-old Winsor organized the Unknowns, a Jamestown ballclub that played the Alleghenies of Warren, the City Club of Erie, the Forest City Club of Cleveland, and other clubs in vacant lots and railroad yards. Though there were no leagues yet, small crowds of curious Jamestowners gathered whenever games were played to see the early incarnations of baseball.

Winsor usually played shortstop and was an excellent hitter. During his school sports visits to towns in Western New York and Pennsylvania, Winsor had learned that baseball was being played elsewhere with a slightly larger ball that led to lower scoring games than those of his childhood at the Flats. Winsor introduced this "dead ball" to Jamestown through his Unknowns, bringing game scores closer to those of modern baseball; scores were lower, games were shorter, and soon more fans came to watch the Unknowns play.

Winsor graduated high school in 1868 and, after two seasons with the Unknowns, left Jamestown to spend the next four years as an umpire in Cleveland and Erie. Winsor returned to Jamestown and was married in 1871 and continued to lead a busy life. Along with inventing a mail-pouch catcher with a partner (the gadget was adopted by most United States railroads), Winsor established the first bottling works in Jamestown in the late 1870s, opened a local factory to manufacture photographic paper, founded the Linford Cut Glass Company, served as Superintendent of Grounds and Buildings of Jamestown Public Schools, was a partner in a grocery store, a member of the Ellicot Hook and Ladder Company, secretary-treasurer of the Jamestown Volunteer Fire Department, and Director of the Cane Seat Chair Company (which burned in one of Jamestown's most spectacular fires).

Winsor died on November 25, 1939 as the last surviving member of the Jamestown High School's class of 1868; he passed away two months after the Baby Bucs finished their first season in the PONY League.

Of all his accomplishments, Winsor's organizing of the Unknowns, and his introduction of the "dead ball" to Jamestown, may be his most lasting. The Unknowns, and the clubs which they spawned, become established in the Jamestown area while other small towns across the country were still largely unfamiliar with baseball. From the earliest days of baseball in America, Jamestown was blessed with the combination of community interest in the game and individuals who promoted the sport locally.

Following the Marlins' inaugural game in Erie, the Expos won their first three games in 1992. Before they could play a fourth, their season was torn apart by tragedy.

Expos trainer Lee Slagle was driving four ballplayers back to Jamestown from a Chautauqua Lake bar early in the morning on June 18 when he lost control of his car. Slagle's car slid 290 feet onto the median of the Southern Tier Expressway, then rolled several times. All five in the car were taken to the hospital where catcher Jim Henderson was listed in serious condition, suffering temporary paralysis from neck and back injuries. Slagle was charged with driving while intoxicated, driving at an unreasonable speed, and an unsafe lane change. He and shortstop Dan Lane were released from the hospital the next day. First baseman Tom Doyle and pitcher Rod Henderson were listed in satisfactory condition and remained under medical attention along with the more seriously injured Jim Henderson.

"He's like my son," said Lowe of Slagle, who was Lowe's assistant trainer at the University of Alabama at Auburn-Montgomery during the college baseball season. "I told the guys God had every chance to take them last night. He must have had a reason why he didn't." Jamestown baseball fans came to the bedside of Henderson with gifts of fruit and magazines while he recovered.

On the field, Lowe's Expos never entirely recovered. Following the accident, they lost seven of eight and went on to finish the season with the worst record in the NY-P League. In the fall, Lowe announced that, for the first time since 1987, he would not return to Jamestown for the next season.

Tim Torricelli, a former player in the Milwaukee Brewers' minor-league system, took over for Lowe. The 1993 Expos rang up an even worse record than the year before. Combined, the 1992 and 1993 clubs won 65 and lost 89 to finish an average of 19 games behind their division leaders.

Far more unsettling than two poor seasons was the pressure major-league baseball owners were putting on minor-league cities throughout the country to upgrade ballparks. A mandate set minimum standards for their minor-league facilities, targeting everything from the height of outfield fences to the width of clubhouse locker rooms.

College Stadium, because of major renovations undertaken in 1984 and 1985, was in better condition than most ballparks. Still, it was estimated that $244,000 would be necessary for major-league-mandated improvements, including new foul poles, new grounds keeping facilities, an expanded "Batter's Eye" in center field, renovation of the home team clubhouse, and a new irrigation system for the outfield.

"Unless something wonderful happens," said Mayor Carolyn Seymour to the *Post-Journal,* "I think we're fooling ourselves." Under the mandate, if Jamestown could not make the costly improvements, College Stadium could no longer serve as home to a major-league affiliate.

Something wonderful didn't happen on October 13, 1993. The Montreal Expos sold the Jamestown Expos to a businessman in Vermont named Ray Pecor, president of the Lake Champlain Transportation Company. Pecor announced that he would move the team to Burlington for the 1994 season. Montreal management never made a profit in Jamestown and wanted to get out of the business of operating a Class A club. In addition, they were pleased to have the team play in Burlington, only an hour away from Montreal.

At least two Jamestown men were not caught by surprise when the move was announced. Local attorney Greg Peterson and Jamestown's "Mr. Baseball" Russ Diethrick were busy trying to rescue minor-league baseball in their home town.

Peterson's life, like Diethrick's, was interwoven with Jamestown professional baseball. As a boy in Jamestown in 1960, he played little-league baseball for coach Duane Shaffer, (Falcon-turned-Oiler) who gave up George Zimmerman's Governor Cup-winning grand slam in 1942. A teammate of Peterson's was a pitcher named Hugh Imus, whose grandfather, Hugh Bedient, watched his games from right field. The manager of Peterson's Babe Ruth League city championship team was John Newman. In high school, Peterson shared a homeroom with John Pollock Jr., son of the former Jamestown Falcons catcher. Peterson played sports with Bob Schmidt, whose father, Dick, threw the first pitch at Municipal Stadium to Pollock.

Peterson went away to college and law school, then returned to Jamestown and met Dan Lunetta. Together, they established an affair between the Montreal Expos organization and The Resource Center, a not-for-profit agency for mentally handicapped and developmentally disabled people. A successful season ticket program resulted in national coverage for

The Resource Center on "This Week in Baseball." In 1988, Peterson arrived late for a "Welcome the Expos" luncheon and was seated with an equally late ballplayer, Marquis Grissom. A summer-long friendship evolved.

On September 1, 1993, almost six weeks before the sale of the Jamestown Expos to Pecor, Greg Peterson interviewed Niagara Falls Rapids manager and former Jamestown Falcons third baseman Larry Parrish as part of an effort to record bits and pieces of local baseball history. Peterson asked Diethrick to join him in general manager Tom O'Reilly's College Stadium office to help direct questions.

Parrish recalled his days in Jamestown, including the first plane ride he ever took—his first trip to Jamestown in 1972—and a "Welcome the Falcons" dinner at which Diethrick was also a guest. "I can remember being so scared," he said. "At that time you don't know how good you are or how you'll do." Peterson and Diethrick asked Parrish about his time in Jamestown, his 15-year major-league career as an All-Star third baseman, and his two years as a player in Japan. Then Parrish interjected one line that would change the course of baseball in Jamestown.

"There have been rumors that our affiliate may be moving down here," said Parrish of the Niagara Falls Rapids. "I don't know if that's true or not or if you guys have heard anything."

Diethrick quietly responded. "It's been talked about a little on the street, yes." The flow of conversation returned to old baseball stories, but Peterson and Diethrick were already thinking ahead.

Soon after the Parrish interview, Peterson spoke with an attorney and friend who worked for Rich Products Corporation, the Buffalo-based company that owned the Niagara Falls Rapids. Niagara Falls' city leaders were having trouble raising the $1.8 million needed to bring Sal Maglie Stadium up to the new major-league-mandated standards and the ownership of the Rapids was wondering if Jamestowners would be interested in housing the franchise. Peterson quickly made contact with Diethrick and Samuel Teresi, the city's Director of Development, who knew the political climate of Jamestown and could help direct negotiations.

When the sale of the Jamestown Expos was announced on Tuesday, October 13, Peterson and his group were free to pursue the Rapids. To alleviate any potential complications that could have been caused by an upcoming mayoral election, Teresi orchestrated a conference call with all three candidates. Each strongly supported the Rapids' potential move to College Stadium.

On Thursday, the NY-P League directors set a deadline of 5 p.m. on Friday for Rich Baseball Operations to make a decision on whether or not to move their franchise to Jamestown. Late the next afternoon, at home plate of College Stadium, the Rich's announced to Mayor Seymour, the City Council, and the press, that they would be moving the Rapids to College Stadium for the 1994 season.

"It's a wonderful and exciting week when on Tuesday you have a buyer for your team and by Friday you have some wonderful new folks who are right in your neighborhood," Mayor Seymour said of the Expos' move to Vermont and the Buffalo-based Rich family.

With Rich Baseball Operations as owners, the city of Jamestown received a total of $430,000 to be used towards College Stadium improvements; the funds came from private donations, New York State's Urban Development Corporation Fund, and the Chautauqua Region Community Foundation.

Niagara Falls, meanwhile, was left flat, as they had been 53 years earlier. "I don't think the impact will be felt until people walk by the stadium on a nice warm summer night," said a Niagara Falls baseball supporter who had fought to keep the Rapids at Sal Maglie Stadium. Niagara Falls, a once-proud industrial city, had fallen on hard times and was living with a 13 percent unemployment rate and a $2 million budget deficit in late 1993. Sal Maglie Stadium was the same park, then known as Hyde Park, that was home to Harry Bisgeier's Niagara

Falls Rainbows in 1939. In 1940, Ernest Kessler brought Bisgeier's poorly attended Rainbows to Jamestown and left Niagara Falls without a minor-league club of their own for 30 years. But an adequate ballpark meant that hope was always alive for a new club to return to Niagara Falls. In 1970, with 1940 Jamestown Falcons pitcher Sal Maglie as general manager, Niagara Falls returned to the NY-P League. The franchise remained there, on and off, until October, 1993.

The Rapids move to College Stadium also meant a homecoming of sorts for the Detroit Tigers, the major-league affiliate for the Rapids. The most notable Tigers employee to enjoy the return to Jamestown was Principal Owner and President, Michael Illitch. The 1952 Falcons infielder from Michigan owned the Tigers and, in 1994, ran the team that would play on the same field where he began his rookie season in baseball. In addition to Illitch, Larry Parrish came back to College Stadium during 1994 as a roving hitting instructor and Wayne Blackburn, twice a replacement manager for Jamestown in the 1950s, was a Detroit scout. Tim Torricelli, released by the Expos after managing the Jamestown club to a last-place finish in 1993, was signed by the Tigers and assigned to Jamestown as hitting coach in 1994.

The Rich's also owned the Buffalo Bisons, so when the Rapids moved to Jamestown the triumvirate of Jamestown-Buffalo-Detroit which was the basis for the success of the Falcons at Municipal Stadium in the 1940s and early 1950s was, in a way, restored.

Another homecoming was that of John McHale Jr. The son of John McHale Sr., who played a large role in keeping baseball in Jamestown during the 1960s and 1970s, McHale Jr. worked as legal counsel for the Expos when his father was president of the Montreal organization in the 1970s. McHale Jr. was later hired as president of the Detroit Tigers and, with the move of the Rapids, was largely responsible for Jamestown's baseball team.

Rich Baseball Operations signed a five-year lease to play at College Stadium and received instant support from the community. The Jamestown Professional Baseball Advisory Council, with Diethrick as chairman and Peterson as president, was formed to work closely with the new club's management to ensure the best interest of professional baseball in Jamestown. A booster club, which elected Flo Wick as their vice president, was established to make the players and their families feel welcome during their stay in town. The boosters would recommend doctors, provide meals to players, and even loan out household items for use during the summer.

Robert E. Rich founded Rich Products Corporation in 1945. The development of Rich's non-dairy Whip Topping—known as "the miracle cream from a soya bean"—helped his business became the nation's largest family-owned frozen foods manufacturer. Rich became well known to Buffalo sports fans when, in 1972, he purchased the naming rights to Erie Country's 80,000 seat football stadium, the home of the Buffalo Bills.

Rich Jr. became involved with Buffalo baseball when Rich Baseball Operations purchased the then-struggling Class AA Bisons franchise. The following year, Rich Jr. led the purchase of the Class AAA Wichita Aeros and switched the two teams' classifications: the Bisons became a Class AAA franchise and the Wichita club became a Class AA franchise. In 1988, Pilot Field was erected in downtown Buffalo and the club's attendance figures soared. Mindy Rich, Rich Jr.'s wife and executive vice president of Rich Baseball Operations, marketed the Bisons to record-breaking attendance marks and earned the 1988 Rawlings Female Executive of the Year award.

Rich Baseball Operations was undoubtedly helped by an explosion in the popularity of minor-league baseball that began in the late 1970s and early 1980s. The reasons are not entirely clear, but the total minor-league attendance figures, which stayed at 10-11 million throughout the late 1960s and 1970s, topped 20 million in 1987 for the first time since

1953. The NY-P League followed the trend. In 1967, the league drew a total of 115,175 fans. In 1991, the NY-P League's attendance soared to 776,185. Even Jamestown's club, which hit a low of 12,840 fans in 1971, rebounded to top 50,000 under general manager Tom Prohaska in 1988.

One of the Rich's first tasks was to choose a name for the Jamestown team, a crucial marketing decision. Over 1,000 entries were submitted, including Mud Bisons, Rich Chaulakers, Lucy Sluggers, Redheads, The Desilous, Furniture Makers, Pearl City Tigers, and Swedes. In the end, Jammers (submitted 47 times) was chosen as the team's new name.

Seven logos were designed by Major League Baseball Properties and one was accepted by Jammers' management—a silver Tasmanian Devil-like creature in a batting stance, bordered by a red and white baseball diamond. To increase merchandising possibilities in an industry where new clubs often outsell established clubs, management decided to follow a trend of introducing two different caps: a solid black one, and a red pinstriped one to be worn by the Jammers only during Sunday games.

A well-placed ad for the caps in *Baseball Weekly* soon brought order requests from 13 different states. "We could have a lousy year in advertising and sell a lot in merchandising," said director of public relations, Doug Sitler. "We're doing a lot of great things at the stadium, but when it boils down to it, baseball is a business."

Rich Baseball Operations' motto was, "Every Game is an Event." Unlike the Montreal Expos, which fielded a team at College Stadium to groom the players for the major leagues, the Rich's came to Jamestown to make money. Jammers' management scheduled a promotion for every single home game of the 1994 season. Among them were "Fireworks Night," "Jamestown Harmony Express Barbershop Chorus Night," the unveiling of a new mascot named J. J. Jammer, and "Italian Fisherman Dixie on the Deck Band Night." Contests included Dickie's Donut Bat Spin, Fountain Bowl

Human Bowling Contest, and The Burger King Whopper Whammer.

"With the promotions we have lined up it will be almost impossible for a fan to leave the stadium without a smile on their face," said the Jammers' vice president.

For better or for worse, the economics of baseball had changed. Promotions and merchandise were making minor-league baseball profitable and, while some pined for the "good old days," professional baseball in Jamestown had the potential to generate income for the first time since the late 1940s.

The 1994 Jammers ended up attracting the second highest number of fans at College Stadium in the last 34 seasons while the minor leagues, as a whole, received generous media attention due to the major-league players' strike.

On the field, the Jammers finished the season tied for first place in their division. They were forced to play a one-game tie-breaker against the Batavia Clippers at College Stadium to determine which team would advance to the playoffs against the McNamara Division winners (also to be decided on the final night of the season).

In front of over 3,000 Jamestown fans, the Clippers scored two runs in the top of the first. The Jammers responded with a run in the bottom of the first when center fielder Mac White tripled and scored on a ground out by Jamestown's Most Valuable Player, right fielder Bubba Trammel (Trammel would make his major-league debut with Detroit in 1997). Trammel doubled and scored in the sixth to tie the game. After the Clippers scored in the top of the ninth, the Jammers again bounced back with a lead-off double, a sacrifice ground out, and a bloop single to center to tie the game at 3-3 and force extra innings.

Meanwhile, Jammers assistant general manager Shawn Reilly was working the phones. While Jamestown and Batavia continued their battle into the 12th inning, the New Jersey Cardinals were playing a doubleheader against the Hudson Valley Renegades in New Jersey. The Cardinals won the first game to edge out the Vermont Expos for the division title, but the second game would determine home-field advantage in the playoffs. If New Jersey lost, the winner of the Batavia-Jamestown game would have the advantage; if the Cardinals won, they would have the advantage.

This all concerned Reilly because, if the Jammers won their game against the Clippers, travel arrangements would need to be made for a game the next night. With time running short, Reilly made hotel reservations in both Vermont and New Jersey. The Cardinals won their second game in 11 innings and chose to play the first playoff game on the road. Therefore, if the Jammers won, game one of their series with the Cardinals would be at College Stadium the next night. Reilly canceled the hotel reservations and called the Jammers' bus driver to tell him that he would not have to make the seven-hour trip to New Jersey later that night.

Reilly was also kept busy moving cases of champagne. When Batavia scored in the top of the ninth to take the lead, the champagne was taken out of the concession stand refrigerator and hauled into the Clippers' locker room. When the Jammers tied the game in the bottom of the ninth, the bottles were removed and put back in the refrigerator. They stayed there into the 12th inning.

In the bottom of the 12th, Jammers second baseman Mike Martin led off with a walk and advanced to second on a wild pitch. Martin then went to third on a sacrifice. With a man on third and one out, the next batter was walked to set up a double play and bring Mac White, who tripled and scored in the first inning, to the plate. White drove the pitch to the center field wall and Martin came home to score.

The Jammers mobbed Martin at home plate and fireworks were set off. "That's the way this team has been all year," said Jammers 33-year-old manager and former major-leaguer, Dave Anderson. "When you think they're down and out, they seem to come up with a run and come back and win. That was no exception tonight."

"I just went nuts," said Flo Wick who was at the game. Afterwards, she and other fans celebrated by going dancing at a local bar.

The next morning, Mac White had to return to the University of South Carolina to begin classes. That night at College Stadium, without White, Trammel slugged a three run homer in the first inning and the Jammers held on to win 3-2 against the Cardinals. The best-of-three playoff series shifted to New Jersey's Skylands Park where the Cardinals won the next two 13-4 and 9-5, despite five more RBI's by Trammel in the series.

A season was over for the Jammers, but Jamestown baseball fans headed into the long off-season knowing that College Stadium would again be home to minor-league baseball the next summer.

Led by a new manager and coaching staff, 25 new players came to Jamestown in 1995, one or two of whom will likely climb to the major leagues. Someday, a few of them may even return to Jamestown to visit old friends, start a new home, or serve the local ballclub in an official capacity.

The people who commit to professional baseball in Jamestown are the ones who will make each season possible, and it is their caring that will continue to make the story of those seasons worthwhile.

APPENDIX A

YEAR	TEAM NAME	BALLPARK	LEAGUE	MAJOR-LEAGUE AFFILIATION
1890-1891	JAMESTOWNS	MARVIN PARK	PENN-NY	
1895	CELORONS	CELORON PARK		
1898	CELORON ACME COLORED GIANTS	CELORON PARK	IRON AND OIL	
1914		CELORON PARK	INTERSTATE	
1915	RABBITS	CELORON PARK	INTERSTATE	
1939	BABY BUCS	CELORON PARK	PONY	PITTSBURGH PIRATES
1940	FALCONS	ALLEN FIELD	PONY	DETROIT TIGERS
1941-1942	FALCONS	MUNICIPAL STADIUM	PONY	DETROIT TIGERS
1943	FALCONS	MUNICIPAL STADIUM	PONY	ST. LOUIS CARDINALS
1944-1956	FALCONS	MUNICIPAL STADIUM	PONY	DETROIT TIGERS
1957	FALCONS	MUNICIPAL STADIUM	NY-P	PITTSBURGH PIRATES
1961-1963	TIGERS	MUNICIPAL STADIUM	NY-P	DETROIT TIGERS
1964	TIGERS	COLLEGE STADIUM	NY-P	DETROIT TIGERS
1965-1966	DODGERS	COLLEGE STADIUM	NY-P	L.A. DODGERS
1967	BRAVES	COLLEGE STADIUM	NY-P	ATLANTA BRAVES
1968-1970	FALCONS	COLLEGE STADIUM	NY-P	BOSTON RED SOX
1971-1973	FALCONS	COLLEGE STADIUM	NY-P	MONTREAL EXPOS
1977-1993	EXPOS	COLLEGE STADIUM	NY-P	MONTREAL EXPOS
1994	JAMMERS	COLLEGE STADIUM	NY-P	DETROIT TIGERS

APPENDIX B

This is a register of every player, coach, and manager to appear on a Jamestown minor-league team roster between the years of 1939 and 1994. If that person appeared on a major-league team roster at any time during his career, the team and the year in which he debuted is also listed.

LAST NAME	FIRST NAME	POSITION	YEAR(S) IN JAMESTOWN
ABREU	MANNY	C	1971
ADAMS	DWAIN	P	1966
ADAMS	KALVIN	INF, OF	1978-79
ADCOCK	BOB	INF	1964
ADKINS	KENNETH	OF	1970
ALEXSON	ANDREW		1946-47
ALFONSECA	ANTONIO (PULPO)	P	1993
Major-League Debut:	1997 Florida Marlins		
ALICOTTA	JOE		1939
ALLEN	MATT	C	1992
ALLEN	RAY	P	1967
ALLEY	JOHN	INF	1972
ALLSWEDE	KEITH	INF	1947-48
ALSNAUER	WILLIAM		1943
ALUSIK	GEORGE	OF	1953
Major-League Debut:	1958 Detroit Tigers		
ANDERSON	SCOTT	P	1977
Major-League Debut:	1983 L. A. Dodgers		
ANDREWS	CHRIS	OF	1955
ANTOINE	WENDELL	C	1956
ANTONETTI	TONY	INF	1973
ARCE	FELIX	OF	1972
ARCHIBALD	DANIEL	P	1989
ARMSTRONG	GEORGE		1944
Major-League Debut:	1946 Philadelphia A's		
ARMSTRONG	IVEY	OF	1966
ATHA			1987

LAST NAME	FIRST NAME	POSITION	YEAR(S) IN JAMESTOWN
ATKINSON	JIM	OF	1979
Major-League Debut:	1976 Montreal Expos		
AUCOIN	DEREK	P	1990
Major-League Debut:	1996 Montreal Expos		
AURICA	BRAD	INF	1992
AVALLONE	PETE	P	1961
AVERS	SCOTT	P	1987
AVERY	KEN		1962
AYERS	STEVE	P	1972-73
BAKER		P	1979
BAKER	DALE	P	1964
BAKER	RICK	P	1972
BALASH	WALT	P	1940-41
BALDRICK	BOB	P	1982
BALSON	AL		1939
BANKOSKI	ALEXANDER		1941
BARBERDO	RUSSELL		1943
BARNES	BRIAN	P	1989
Major-League Debut:	1990 Montreal Expos		
BARNETT	DAVE	OF	1979
BARNHARDT	ROBERT	INF	1939
BARNHART		INF	1945
BARON		OF	1947
BARR	DICK	P	1952
BARR	STEVE	P	1969
Major-League Debut:	1974 Boston Red Sox		
BARRY	JEFF	OF	1990
Major-League Debut:	1995 Montreal Expos		
BARTON	DAVID	INF, OF, P	1970
BARTOZEK	JOHN		1941
BARTZ	THEODORE	OF	1945-46
BASS	JASON	OF	1994
BASTIAN	JOSE	P	1973
BATES	BILL	P	1967
BATISTA	JUAN	INF	1993
BAXTER	ROBERT	P	1990

LAST NAME	FIRST NAME	POSITION	YEAR(S) IN JAMESTOWN
BAYS	DICK	P	1954
BECK	STANLEY	P	1969-70
BEEBE	KEN	P	1972
BELL	ED	OF	1977
BENEDICT	MOBY	MGR	1982
BENEFIEL	DOUGLAS	C	1992
BENENATI		OF	1947
BENITEZ	YAMIL	OF	1992
Major-League Debut:	1995 Montreal Expos		
BENTFIELD	DICK	INF	1951
BENZA	AL	INF	1953
BERARDINO	RICHARD	COACH	1968-69
BERBELK	MARV	P	1961
BERG	MIKE	INF	1969
BERGALOWSKI	CHET	C	1967
BERGERON	GILLES	P	1987
BERGSTROM	WILBUR		1941
BERMINGHAM	ALBERT		1943
BERRIER	BILL	MGR	1966
BERSIN	MIKE	INF	1967
BETUSH	ED	P	1963
BIAGINI	GREG	INF	1973
BIRRER	WILLIAM (BABE)	P	1947
Major-League Debut:	1955 Detroit Tigers		
BISHOP	CHARLES	P	1943
Major-League Debut:	1952 Philadelphia A's		
BLACK	JOSEPH	P	1939
BLACK	WILLIAM	P	1939
BLACKBURN	WAYNE	MGR, OF	1954, 1956
BLACKWELL	TIM	C	1970
Major-League Debut:	1974 Boston Red Sox		
BLAIR	DENNIS	P	1972
Major-League Debut:	1974 Montreal Expos		
BLANCHARD	ROBERT	INF	1940
BLISS	LYLE	P	1944-45
BLOOM	ROBERT	P	1951

LAST NAME	FIRST NAME	POSITION	YEAR(S) IN JAMESTOWN
BLOWERS	MIKE	INF	1986
Major-League Debut:	1989 N. Y. Yankees		
BLY	JOHN	OF	1962
BOEING	THOMAS		1940
BOLDEN	BILL	P	1971-72
BOLLING	FRANK	INF	1951
Major-League Debut:	1954 Detroit Tigers		
BONIFACE	GEORGE		1943
BONK		INF	1971
BORISH	JIM	INF	1968
BOROWICZ	STANLEY	OF	1941
BOTEZE	CARL	P	1968-69
BRADLEY	ALBERT	INF	1940-41
BRADLEY	DICK	C	1973
BRADSHAW	PAUL	OF	1965
BREWER	BILLY	P	1990
BRIAN	BRAD	C	1987
BRITO	MARIO	P	1987
BRITTAN	CALVIN		1944
BRODEUR	CLAUDE	P	1981
BROMMER	GEORGE	P	1961
BROOKS		P	1947
BROOKS	JEROME	P	1944
BROWN	ISAAC (IKE)	INF	1962
Major-League Debut:	1969 Detroit Tigers		
BRYANT	DONALD	C	1962
Major-League Debut:	1966 Chicago Cubs		
BRYANT	GARY	P	1973
BRYANT	JIM	P	1969-70
BRYERS			1948
BRYKET	BLAKE	P	1979-80
BULLOCK	JOSH	P	1993
BUMGARTNER	JOHN	OF	1950
BUNTING	HOWARD		1940
BURANSKAS	VICTOR	INF	1947
BURKE	DON	OF	1986

LAST NAME	FIRST NAME	POSITION	YEAR(S) IN JAMESTOWN
BURKE	JOHN	P	1943
BURNETT	GARY	P	1972
BURT	RICHARD N.	C	1951
BUTTERS	TOM	P	1957
Major-League Debut:	1962 Pittsburgh Pirates		
BUYS	BRUCE	P	1965
BUZZARD	DALE	P	1989
BUZZINOTTI	GRENO		1939
CABADAS	ART	P	1963-64
CABALLERO	BOB	OF	1970
CAHILL	JAMES	INF	1945
CAMARENA	JUAN	P	1971
CAMBURN	BOB	OF	1965
CAMPOS	JESUS	OF	1993
CARBALLO	PABLO	INF	1977
CARDINAL	CONRAD (RANDY)	P	1962
Major-League Debut:	1963 Houston Astros		
CARDONA	JAVIER	C	1994
CARINO	SKIP	C	1968
CARLSON	IRVING	INF	1947
CARMICHAEL	EDWARD		1939
CARNEGIE	OLIVER	OF, MGR	1944
CARNEVALE	DAN	MGR	1953
Major-League Debut:	1970 Cleveland Indians		
CARRIER	LANNIE	INF	1963
CARRION	LEONEL	COACH	1986
CARSWELL	FRANK	INF	1941
Major-League Debut:	1953 Detroit Tigers		
CARTER	JEFF	P	1987
Major-League Debut:	1991 Chicago White Sox		
CARTER	ROBERT		1943
CASABLANCA	FERNANDO	INF	1969-70
CASKEY	CRAIG	P	1972
Major-League Debut:	1973 Montreal Expos		
CASTRO	JOSE	COACH	1990
CASWELL	MARV		1956

LAST NAME	FIRST NAME	POSITION	YEAR(S) IN JAMESTOWN
CATAL	TOM	P	1967
CATES	TIM	P	1979-80
CAUCCI	RAY	OF	1961-62
CAVALLER	KEVIN	P	1987
CERNICH	JOE	OF	1964
CHAPPIE	DON	INF, P	1947-49
CHESSER	BRANDON	P	1981
CHESTER	ALLEN	P	1952
CHURLHICH	BOB	INF	1967
CIAGLO	PAUL	P	1989
CIANFROCCO	ANGEL (ARCHI)	INF	1987
Major-League Debut:	1992 Montreal Expos		
CICARELL	GEORGE		1939
CIESLA	TED	INF	1990
CIPOLLA	MITCH	C	1977
CLARK	RICKEY	P	1965
Major-League Debut:	1967 California Angels		
CLEMO	SCOTT	INF	1986
CLENDENNON	DONN	INF	1957
Major-League Debut:	1961 Pittsburgh Pirates		
CLOUTIER	MIKE	INF	1961
COCCITTI	CHARLES		1943
COLEMAN	PAUL		1940
COLLINS	BOB	P	1950
COLLINS	MIKE	P	1968-69
COLVIN	WILLIAM	INF	1943
CONLAN	HARRY	OF	1971
CONQUAY	EUGENE B	P	1950
COOLEY	WILLIE	OF	1981
COOPER	CECIL	INF	1968
Major-League Debut:	1971 Boston Red Sox		
COPPOL	WALT	P	1978
CORCORAN	HAROLD	P	1943
CORDERO	WIL	INF	1988
Major-League Debut:	1992 Montreal Expos		
COREY	BRYAN	INF	1994

LAST NAME	FIRST NAME	POSITION	YEAR(S) IN JAMESTOWN
CORLESS	MAX	P	1947-48
CORNISH	JOE	OF	1964
CORREA	JUAN	INF	1971
CORRIGAN	BILL	P	1966
COTT	ORVAL	INF	1946
COULON	TIM	C	1967
COVLE	MEADE	INF	1940
COWAN	GARY	C	1961
COX	GREG	P	1977-78
CRAWFORD	DOUG	INF	1966
CRAWFORD	JOHN		1939
CRAWFORD	WILLIAM D.	INF	1949
CRESPO	MANNY	INF	1968
CRESSMAN	ROBERT	P	1962
CROKEN	BILL	C	1969
CRORY	FRED	P	1943
CROSS	CHRIS	C	1968
CUCCURULLO	ART	P	1940
CUMMINGS	DICK	P	1961
CUNNINGHAM	MARK	INF	1973
CUPP	BILL	OF	1967
CURAN	JOSEPH		1940
CURTIS	DISHMAN	INF	1982
DALTON	DENNIS	P	1967
DAMON	JOHN	INF	1981
DANCHIK	JOHN	P	1969
DARAGON	BOB	INF	1978
DARNELL	DALE	OF	1968
DASILVA	FERNANDO	P	1993
DAUGHERTY	JERRY	C	1969-70
DAUGHERTY	PAT	MGR	1977-81, 1990
DAVIDSON	SCOTT	INF	1989
DAVIE	JERRY	P	1952
Major-League Debut:	1959 Detroit Tigers		
DAVIS	GLENN	INF	1964

LAST NAME	FIRST NAME	POSITION	YEAR(S) IN JAMESTOWN
DAVIS	OTIS	OF	1943
Major-League Debut:	1946 Brooklyn Dodgers		
DAWES	STEVE	INF	1981
DEAN	JERRY	P	1951
DEBOEVER	BILL	P	1986
DECRUYDT	A.	P	1948
DEFUSCO			1944
DEKAY	ROBERT B.	OF	1948-49
DELAZZER	ROGER	OF	1973
DELONG	TOM	OF	1965
DENNING	SHAMROCK		1943
DENNO	ROBERT		1939
DEPILLO	GEORGE		1948
DESHIELDS	DELINO		1987
Major-League Debut:	1990 Montreal Expos		
DIAZ	RALPH	P	1990
DIETZ	JIM	INF	1961
DILAURO	JACK	P	1963
Major-League Debut:	1969 N. Y. Mets		
DIMITRIADIS	JIMMY	P	1946
DINKEL	MATT	P	1973
DISHMAN	CURTIS	INF	1982
DOBBERSTEIN	ARTHUR	C	1945
DOBSON	PAT	P	1963
Major-League Debut:	1967 Detroit Tigers		
DOLMAN	DONALD		1939
DONNER	GLEN	P	1977-78
DOPSON	JOHN	P	1982
Major-League Debut:	1985 Montreal Expos		
DORISH	HARRY	MGR	1967
Major-League Debut:	1947 Boston Red Sox		
DORSEY	ROBERT T.	C	1949
DOSS	LARRY	OF	1987
DOSTALER	MIKE	P	1971
DOTSON	HARDY	OF	1981-82
DOYLE	TOM	INF	1992

LAST NAME	FIRST NAME	POSITION	YEAR(S) IN JAMESTOWN
DREIFORT	TODD	OF	1992
DRIGGERS	JAMIE	P	1964
DRISKELL	JEFF	C	1994
DRUMWRIGHT	DAVE	P	1972
DUDLEY	DON	P	1970
DUEY	KODY	INF	1986
DUFFIE	JOHN	P	1966
Major-League Debut:	1967 L. A. Dodgers		
DUKE	DOUG	C	1986
DUSTAL	BOB	P	1955
Major-League Debut:	1963 Detroit Tigers		
DWYER	ALAN		1955
DZITKO	VINCENT	P	1970
EAGAN	STEVE	C	1968
EATON	DICK	INF	1950
EDDY	DE LA CRUZ	OF	1973
EDGAR	JAMES	C	1943
EDGE	LEO	P	1969
EDMUNDS	TED	P	1950
EDWARDS	RANDOLPH	P	1943-45
EGGERS	LES	OF	1947
EGGERT	DAVID	P	1992
ELDER	ISSAC	OF	1989
ELDRIDGE	TERRY	OF	1981
ELEY	GEORGE		1939
ENGELKEN	GARY	COACH	1989
ENRIGHT	BENJAMIN		1944
ERICKSON	BURWIN	P	1946-47
ESTERMYER	WIBBI	INF	1955
EVANS	EARL	P	1944-46
EVANS	DWIGHT	OF	1969
Major-League Debut:	1972 Boston Red Sox		
EVANS	LARRY	P	1971-72
EVERETT	FRED	P	1950
EVERRET	ED	P	1966
FALK	THOMAS C.	INF	1949

LAST NAME	FIRST NAME	POSITION	YEAR(S) IN JAMESTOWN
FALLS	RON	P	1968
FALTEISEK	STEVE	P	1992
FANO	LEO		1945
FARMER	HOWARD	P	1987
Major-League Debut:	1990 Montreal Expos		
FARRELL	MIKE	P	1977
FARRINGTON	JERRY		1962
FAUTH	JOHN	INF	1948
FAUTH	LEW	P	1947
FEDAK	MICKEY	P	1962-63
FEDEROFF	ALFRED	INF	1946-47, 1961
Major-League Debut:	1951 Detroit Tigers		
FEKETE	JAMES	P	1961
FERGUSON	JAMES	P	1992
FERRIS	DALE W.	P	1951
FIALKO	EDWARD		1941
FICKINGER	JOHN	P	1952
FIELD	DAN	C	1971-72
FIELDS	BRUCE	OF	1986
Major-League Debut:	1986 Detroit Tigers		
FINLAY	ANDY	OF	1967
FINNERTY		INF	1971
FITZPATRICK	ROB	C	1990
FLEMING	JIM	COACH	1992
FLETCHER	JOHN	C	1969
FLEURY	DENNIS	INF	1977
FLINT	ELBURT		1944
FLOWERS	DAVID	P	1979
FONSECA	JUAN	C	1973
FORD	SID	C	1951
FORD	TOM	P	1973
FORNARI	JOHN	C	1948
FORTSON	RALPH	OF	1955
FORTUNE	DICK	P	1950
FOSTER	JEFF	INF	1993
FOX	KEN	OF	1986

LAST NAME	FIRST NAME	POSITION	YEAR(S) IN JAMESTOWN
FOX	NELSON J. (NELLIE)	OF	1944
Major-League Debut:	1947 Philadelphia A's		
FRANKLIN	WILBERT	OF	1963
FRANKS	PAUL	P	1952-53
FRANSON	ART	P	1973
FREEMAN	SEAN	INF	1994
FREMING	JAMES		1940
FREMMING	KEN	P	1947-48
FRIEDLAND	MIKE	INF	1990
FURLONG	WILLIAM D.	P	1949
GALARRAGA	ANDRE	C, OF, INF	1981
Major-League Debut:	1985 Montreal Expos		
GALBATO	CHAN	P	1986
GALBREATH	RON	P	1981
GARCIA	LUIS	INF	1994
GARDNER	MARK	P	1985
Major-League Debut:	1989 Montreal Expos		
GAVILLIAN	PEDRO	C	1977, 1979
GAYLOR	ROBERT	INF	1986
GAYNOR	DAVE	INF	1973
GENTILE	SCOTT	P	1992
GEORGE	JERRY	INF	1978
GEOTCH	ARTHUR	P	1943
GERA	STEPHEN		1939
GILBERT	DENNY	OF	1968
GILMORE	JAMES	INF	1944
GIMINIANI	DICK	P	1963
GINSBURG	MYRON (JOE)	C	1944
Major-League Debut:	1948 Detroit Tigers		
GINSTE	WAYNE	INF	1965
GLYNN	GENE	INF, MGR	1979, 1986-87
Major-League Debut:	1994 Colorado Rockies		
GODFREY	MURRAY	P	1968
GONALEZ	HECTOR	INF, OF	1971
GONZALES	DAN	OF	1978
GOOD	FRANNIE	INF	1950

LAST NAME	FIRST NAME	POSITION	YEAR(S) IN JAMESTOWN
GOODELL	GEORGE	INF	1939
GOODMAN	BOB	C	1972
GOOKIN	CLIFFORD (RED)	P	1950, 1952
GRACIA	HENRY	INF	1968
GRANGER	TONY	P	1961
GRANT	RICK	INF	1967
GRAPENTHIN	DICK	P	1980
Major-League Debut:	1983 Montreal Expos		
GRAVES	ROBERT	P	1981
GREWAL	RANBIR	P	1990
GRIFFIN	HANK	OF	1968
GRINRICH	GARY	INF	1973
GRISSOM	MARQUIS	OF	1988
Major-League Debut:	1989 Montreal Expos		
GRONLUND	DAVE	P	1973
GRUBB	CHRIS	INF	1993
GRUDZIELANEK	MARK	INF	1991
Major-League Debut:	1995 Montreal Expos		
GRZENDA	JOE	P	1955
Major-League Debut:	1961 Detroit Tigers		
GUTIERREZ	MIKE	OF	1967
GUTIERREZ	RICO	OF	1967
GUTSHALL	HOWIE	OF	1948
GUZMAN	ISMAEL	OF	1994
HAAR	RICH	INF	1993
HAGGERTY	PAT	OF	1948
HAGGITT	LARRY	INF	1965
HAINES	MIKE	P	1986
HALL			1982
HALL	DAVE	OF	1977
HALL	PERRY		1939
HALL	TOM	OF	1971
HAMILTON	JACK	INF	1969
HAMONS	LOWELL	P	1944
HAMRICK	CONNIE	INF	1961
HAND		P	1947

LAST NAME	FIRST NAME	POSITION	YEAR(S) IN JAMESTOWN
HANDEL	LONNIE	C	1968, 1970
HANEY	CHRIS	P	1990
Major-League Debut:	1991 Montreal Expos		
HANSEN	TEREL	OF	1987
HARBOUR	BILL	P	1952
HARDIN	WILBUR	OF	1941
HARDY	MARK	OF	1986
HARGIS	DAN	C	1990
HARNICK	WILLIAM	OF	1940
HARRELL	MATT	C	1993
HARRISON	SCOTT	P	1992-93
HART	GARY	P	1964-65
HART	MIKE	INF	1972
HARTMAN	EARL		1943
HARTSELL		P	1947-48
HARTSOCK	GARY	P	1978-79
HARVISON	MIKE	OF	1968-69
HATFIELD	DICK	P	1952
HATFIELD	FRED	MGR	1963
Major-League Debut:	1950 Boston Red Sox		
HAVEN	D.		1948
Haynes	Heath	P	1991
Major-League Debut:	1994 Montreal Expos		
HAZARD	DICK	OF	1962
HEARN	BARNEY	OF	1944-45
HEFFNER	DAVE	INF, OF	1973
HEIDERSCHEIT	PAT	P	1989
HEIDORN	RICH	INF	1977
HEIN	STEWART	OF	1953
HELD	HERSHEL	P	1943
HELLER	FRANK	INF	1940-41
HENDERSON	CHARLES		1939
HENDERSON	JIM	C	1992
HENDERSON	ROD	P	1992
HENLEY	GAIL	MGR	1965
Major-League Debut:	1954 Pittsburgh Pirates		

LAST NAME	FIRST NAME	POSITION	YEAR(S) IN JAMESTOWN
HENLEY	ROBERT	C	1993
HENNINGHAM	AL	P	1955-56
HENRY	MARK	OF	1981
HERSTEK	WILLIAM	P	1945
HERTEL	JOSEPH		1943
HERTZLER	PAUL	INF	1981
HESINIUS	ROBERT	P	1943
HETMAN	MIKE	C	1970
HETZ	GEORGE J.	INF	1950-51
HEWITT	TONY	INF	1972
HICKS	KENNETH	P	1944
HILL	NORWOOD	P	1969
HILLER	JACK	P	1963
Major-League Debut:	1965 Detroit Tigers		
HIMES	RALPH	P	1939
HINTON	RUSS	INF	1962
HIRSCH	CHRIS	C	1990
HOCUTT	MIKE	INF	1982
HOLMAN	BRIAN	P	1983
Major-League Debut:	1988 Montreal Expos		
HOLMES	CHARLES		1943
HOLMES	JACK	P	1944
HOLMQUIST	DOUG	C	1964
Major-League Debut:	1984 N. Y. Yankees		
HOLODICK	MIKE	INF	1963-64
HOLTZ	JOSEPH	P	1940
HOMS	IRV	C	1972
HOOKS	LORENZO	P	1978
HOPKINS	DON	OF	1972
Major-League Debut:	1975 Oakland A's		
HOPKINS	MIKE	P	1978
HOSKINS	MARK	INF	1944-45
HRINIAK	WALTER	MGR	1972-73
Major-League Debut:	1968 Atlanta Braves		
HROVATIC	ERNEST	OF	1943
HUBBARD	DAVE	OF	1970

LAST NAME	FIRST NAME	POSITION	YEAR(S) IN JAMESTOWN
HUBER		P	1979
HUBER	RANDY	P	1981
HUDSON	DERICK	OF	1989
HUGHES	CHUCK	INF	1964
HUGHES	RICKY	OF	1973
HUMPHREY	KENNETH	OF	1945-46
HUNTER	JIM	P	1985
Major-League Debut:	1991 Milwaukee Brewers		
HURDLE		C	1943
HURST	THOMAS	P	1946
ILLITCH	MIKE	INF	1952
IRACE	JOHN	INF	1954
IRELAND	CHARLES		1939
IRELAND	TIMOTHY	INF	1973
Major-League Debut:	1981 Kansas City Royals		
ISHMAEL	MIKE	INF	1987
IVY	DAVID	INF	1970
JACKSON	ALAN	P	1970
JACKSON	CHARLIE	P	1971
JACOBS	DICK	P	1968
JACOBSON	NELS	P	1986
JACOBSON	WILLIAM		1943
JAMES	CHARLES	P	1943
JAMES	LES		1939
JAMISON	WALTER	P	1944
JARVIS	PAT	P	1961
Major-League Debut:	1966 Atlanta Braves		
JAVIER	JULIAN		1957
JEAN	ARCHIE	OF	1991
JELLISON	GARY	P	1967
JENKINS	BRETT	INF	1991
JENKINS	CLYDE	P	1970
JENNINGS			1939
JENSEN	JACKIE	MGR	1970
Major-League Debut:	1950 N. Y. Yankees		
JOHNS	DAN	P	1977

LAST NAME	FIRST NAME	POSITION	YEAR(S) IN JAMESTOWN
JOHNSON	CHARLIE	INF	1950
JOHNSON	GARY	P	1964
JOHNSON	GREG	P	1980-81
JOHNSON	HENRY A.	P	1949-50
JOHNSON	MIKE	OF	1968-69
JOHNSON	RANDY	P	1985
Major-League Debut:	1988 Montreal Expos		
JOHNSON	RAY	C	1966
JOHNSON	ROY	OF	1979
JOHNSON	TED	OF	1966
JOHNSON	TONY	OF	1977
Major-League Debut:	1981 Montreal Expos		
JOHNSON	WALLACE	INF	1979-80
Major-League Debut:	1981 Montreal Expos		
JOINER	TERRY	INF, P	1969-70
JOK	STANLEY	P	1971
JONAS	LUIS	INF	1973
JONES	ANSON	INF	1984
JONES	DICK	P	1956
JONES	WALTER	P	1966
JORDON	MILTON	P	1948
Major-League Debut:	1953 Detroit Tigers		
JOSEPH	TONY	P	1962
JOSEPHSON	PAUL	P	1978
KAISER	HOWARD	P	1943
KAM	HERBERT		1939-40
KAPUSCINSKI	TED	P	1947
KAREKA	CHESTER		1942
KARLIK	EMIL	OF	1951
KATZAROFF	ROBBIE	OF	1990
KAUB	KEITH	INF	1988
KAUTS	GEORGE		1943
KAZAKAVICH	BERNIE	P	1961-62
KEECH	GEORGE	OF	1965
KEENER	JOE	P	1973
KELLOG	KERRY	P	1979-80

LAST NAME	FIRST NAME	POSITION	YEAR(S) IN JAMESTOWN
KEMP	MILAN W.	INF	1948-49
KERNS	RUSSELL	C	1946-47
Major-League Debut:	1945 Detroit Tigers		
KERR	CLIFF	P	1971
KERRIGAN	ROBERT	P	1987-88
KILGO	RAY	P	1989
KIMP		P	1945
KING	CHARLES (CHICK)	OF	1951
Major-League Debut:	1954 Detroit Tigers		
KING	REGGIE	C	1982
KING	STEPHEN	P	1986
KINNS	GLENN	P	1982
KIRKPATRICK	TOM	P	1955
KLAENER	EDWARD		1940
KLANCNIK	JOE	P	1989
KLEINSMITH	GERALD	P	1948
KLIS	STANLEY	P	1944
KNABE		P	1950
KNIEPPER	AARON	P	1993
KOBUSKIE	JACK		1944
KOBY	GEORGE	P	1943
KOEYERS	RAMSEY	C	1993
KOLEFF	NICK		1954-55
KOPLITZ	HOWARD	P	1956
Major-League Debut:	1961 Detroit Tigers		
KORINCE	GEORGE	P	1965
Major-League Debut:	1966 Detroit Tigers		
KOSCHAK	SETH	C	1970
KOSHOREK	CLEMENT	INF	1946
KOSTRO	FRANK	INF	1956
Major-League Debut:	1962 Detroit Tigers		
KOTCH	DARRIN	P	1990
KOUNS	WILLIAM	P	1970
KRAMER	TOM	C	1969
KRIST	ALLEN		1939
KUCKER	WILLIAM		1940

LAST NAME	FIRST NAME	POSITION	YEAR(S) IN JAMESTOWN
KURT	LINDY		1962
KURTZMAN	HAL	INF	1969
KWICINSKI	MIKE	INF	1981
KYES	ROBERT		1943, 1948
LA CHANCE	VINCENT	OF	1993
LA FRANCOIS	ROGER	MGR	1988
Major-League Debut:	1982 Boston Red Sox		
LA LONGE	LEWIS		1943
LA LONGE	MICKEY	MGR	1939
LA ROSE	JOHN	P	1970
LAKE	KEN	OF	1988-89
LAKER	TIMOTHY	C	1988-89
Major-League Debut:	1992 Montreal Expos		
LANDRETH	LARRY	P	1973
Major-League Debut:	1976 Montreal Expos		
LANDRY	LONNY	OF	1994
LANE	DANNY	INF	1992
LANGE	JACK		1939
LANTIGVA		C	1971
LAROSA	MARK	P	1991
LARSEN	EARL		1940
LARSON	GAIL R.	INF	1949
LARSON	LEE	INF	1967
LARY	FRANK	P	1950
Major-League Debut:	1954 Detroit Tigers		
LAU	CHARLIE	C	1952
Major-League Debut:	1956 Detroit Tigers		
LAUZIERE	MIKE	OF	1981-82
LAWRENCE	RAYMOND	INF	1939
LAZAROU	ARISTOTLE	P	1943
LEBRON	JUSTO	OF	1973
LEE	CHARLES	OF	1992
LEEDER	JAMES (JOE)	P	1971-73
LEGGITT	ERIC	OF	1982
LEMON	RICKY	OF	1981-82
LEMONE	NICK	INF	1940

LAST NAME	FIRST NAME	POSITION	YEAR(S) IN JAMESTOWN
LEON	DANILLO	P	1987
LERCHEN	GEORGE	OF	1942, 1946
Major-League Debut:	1952 Detroit Tigers		
LETCHWORTH	WILLIAM	P	1951
LEVEY	JIM	INF, MGR	1945
Major-League Debut:	1930 St. Louis Browns		
LEWIS	BILL	P	1964
LEYLAND	JIM	C, P	1965
Major-League Debut:	1970 Detroit Tigers		
LICINI	DICK	INF	1969
LINCOLN	DANIEL	P	1945
LIND	THOMAS		1944
LISIECKI	RICHARD	INF	1951-52, 1954-55
LITTLE	BRYAN		1980
Major-League Debut:	1982 Montreal Expos		
LITWHILER	DANIEL	MGR	1954
Major-League Debut:	1940 Philadelphia Phillies		
LOCKMAN	CHARLES	OF	1943
LOEFFLER	BUZZ	C	1979
LOGAN	JOSEPH	P	1989
LONG	JOHN		1940
LONG	STEVE	P	1990
LOONEY	BRIAN	P	1991
Major-League Debut:	1993 Montreal Expos		
LOPES	H. J.	INF	1984
LOPEZ	JIM	INF	1964-65
LOWE	LLOYD	INF	1943
LOWE	Q. V.	COACH, MGR	1987-92
LUGOS	FRANK	P	1943
LUKON	JOHN	INF	1939
LUMADVE	JIM	INF, OF	1952, 1955-56
LUMLEY	DON	INF, OF	1954-55
LUMPE	JIM	INF	1982
LUND	DON	MGR	1956
Major-League Debut:	1945 L. A. Dodgers		
LUNDEEN	BILL	P	1964

LAST NAME	FIRST NAME	POSITION	YEAR(S) IN JAMESTOWN
LUPIEN	TONY	INF, MGR	1951-52, 1955
Major-League Debut:	1940 Boston Red Sox		
LYONS	BOB	P	1961
MAAS	JACK (DUKE)	P	1950
Major-League Debut:	1951 Detroit Tigers		
MACALASTER	BRUCE	INF	1977
MACHACEK	KEN	P	1986
MACK	WALTER		1940
MACKASEY	BLAIR	OF	1973
MACLI	ALFRED		1945
MACON	MAX	MGR	1963
Major-League Debut:	1938 St. Louis Card's		
MAGLIE	SALVATORE	P	1940
Major-League Debut:	1945 N. Y. Giants		
MAGOWN	KEN	P	1961
MAHER	BUDDY	P	1979
MAHLER	GARY	INF	1983-84
MALINOWSKI	JOE	INF	1950
MALONE	KEVIN	COACH	1988
MANNERINO	FRANK	OF	1968
MARCHAND	RENE	INF	1981
MARCHOK	CHRIS	P	1987
MARCO	GUS	P	1964
MARQUETTE	GEORGE	INF	1948
MARSDEN	JOHN	P	1969
MARTIN		P	1987
MARTIN	MICHAEL	INF	1994
MARTINEAU	PAUL	INF	1986
MARTINEZ	DALVIS	INF	1994
MARVELE	MIKE	OF	1973
MASON	FELTON	OF	1989
MASON	KIM	P	1977
MATHILE	MICHAEL	P	1990
MATOS	DOMINGO	INF	1990-91
MAY	LENNY	OF	1981
MAYO	TODD	OF	1989

LAST NAME	FIRST NAME	POSITION	YEAR(S) IN JAMESTOWN
MAZERALL	MIKE	P	1968
MAZEROSKI	DARREN	INF	1984
MCCAMMON	DAVE	OF	1966
MCCARTY	WILLIAM		1940
MCCLUSKEY	AUSTIN	P	1950
MCCONNELL	JOHN	C, INF	1978
MCCUBBIN	SHANE	C	1992
MCDONALD	JAMES	P	1986
MCELROY	FRANK	INF	1953
MCFARLAND	DALE E.	INF	1950
MCGREEVY	STEVE	INF	1966
MCHUGH	SCOTT	INF	1987
MCNAIR	PAT	INF	1942
MCNEILANCE	ALEX D.	P	1949
MCNULTY	EDMOND	P	1951
MCSWEEN	DENIS	P	1971
MEDLAR	CHARLES	P	1942
MEE	RALPH		1939
MEELER	PHIL	P	1968
Major-League Debut:	1972 Detroit Tigers		
MEINTS	VERNON	P	1943
MELAGO	JOE	OF	1952
MELTON	STEVE	INF	1973
MENA	VADA		1962
MENOON	KEVIN	P	1978
MEYER		P	1945
MEYERS	WILLIAM	OF	1963
MIALI	JAMES	OF	1963
MIELKO	JOHN	INF	1944
MILLER	BOB	P	1964
MILLER	JACK	P	1951
MILLER	RICK	P	1982-83
MINARCK	WILLIAM		1944
MINNIS	VIRL	INF, C	1944-45
MISCHE	BOB	P	1953-54
MITCHELL	FRED	P	1982

LAST NAME	FIRST NAME	POSITION	YEAR(S) IN JAMESTOWN
MITCHELL	JORGE	OF	1987-88
MITCHELL	TOM	C	1966
MITSCHELE	CLAUDE	P	1952
MODAK	MIKE	P	1943
Major-League Debut:	1945 Cincinnati Reds		
MOKAN	LEONARD	OF	1941
MONROE	DARRYL	OF	1994
MONTGOMERY	DON		1983
MONTGOMERY	TOM	P	1979
MOORE	BARRY	P	1964
MOORE	JACKIE	MGR	1968-69
Major-League Debut:	1965 Detroit Tigers		
MOORING	JIM	INF	1962, 1964
MORALES	NEVDO	INF	1967
MORDARSKI	EDWARD	C	1944
MORENEWEG	WILLIAM	OF	1944
MORENO	CARLOS	P	1967
MORGAN	DAN	P	1977-78
MORGAN	DAVE	P	1966
MORGAN	JACK	OF	1950
MORGAN	WILLIS	P	1944
MORRIS	FRED		1943
MORROW	DAVID	C	1986
MORROW	DONALD K.	INF	1949
MORTON	BUBBA	INF	1956
Major-League Debut:	1961 Detroit Tigers		
MOSS	STAN	INF	1968
MOSTAK	JOHN	P	1950
MOULDER	FRED	INF	1966
MOVA	FELIX	P	1990
MOYER	ROBERT	INF	1944
MUCHA	AL	P	1939
MULLEAVY	GREG	INF, MGR	1941-42
Major-League Debut:	1930 Chicago White Sox		
MULLIN	PAT	MGR	1956
Major-League Debut:	1940 Detroit Tigers		

LAST NAME	FIRST NAME	POSITION	YEAR(S) IN JAMESTOWN
MUNGER	CHARLES	P	1940
MURRAY	FLOYD	P	1966
MURRAY	GLENN	OF	1990
Major-League Debut:	1996 Philadelphia Phillies		
MURRAY	LEO	P	1939
MYRAH	JIM	P	1967
NATAL	ROB	C	1987
Major-League Debut:	1992 Montreal Expos		
NAVARRO	HENRY	INF	1950
NEAL	MIKE	P	1968
NEALEIGH	ROD	OF	1980
NEDELCO	AL	P	1946
NEEBLING	BOB	P	1952
NEELY	LYLE	OF, P	1944-45
NEUBERGER	WARREN	P	1953
NEWARD	DONALD		1939
NEWBY	KEVIN	OF	1977
NEWELL		OF	1973
NEWMAN	EVERETT	P	1962-63
NEWMAN	JOHN	OF, C	1940-42
NEWTON	BILL	P	1965
NEWTON	BOB	INF	1955
NICHOLS	JOSEPH W.	P	1949
NICHOLSON	HARVEY		1946
NICHTING	TIM	C	1982
NIELSEN	CHAD	INF	1970
NORMENT	MIKE	C	1981
NORRIS	JOE	P	1990
NORTHRUP	KEVIN	OF	1992
NORTON	BILL	INF	1969
NORTON	CHRIS	INF	1992
NORTON	RANDY	P	1983
NORWOOD	DAVE	P	1968
NOWAK	HENRY	OF	1940
NOWLIN	DON	INF	1969
NUTTER	JACK	P	1964

LAST NAME	FIRST NAME	POSITION	YEAR(S) IN JAMESTOWN
NYILAS	AY		1939
NYMAN	JERRY	OF	1990
O'BRIEN	DON	C	1955
O'BRIEN	PHIL	P	1966
O'CONNOR	CLARENCE	OF	1950
O'CONNOR	JACK	P	1977
Major-League Debut:	1981 Minnesota Twins		
O'NEIL	DOUG	OF	1991
O'NEIL	JOHN	INF, MGR	1941, 1954
Major-League Debut:	1946 Philadelphia Phillies		
O'ROURKE	JOE	MGR	1940
Major-League Debut:	1929 Philadelphia Phillies		
OFFENHAMMER	RICHARD	C	1940
OGLIVIE	BEN	INF	1968
Major-League Debut:	1971 Boston Red Sox		
OLIVER	DON	P	1980
OLIVEROS	ROMULO	C	1984
OLLER	JEFF	INF	1986
OLSON	MARVIN	MGR	1945-49
Major-League Debut:	1931 Boston Red Sox		
OROPEZA	DAVE	P	1988
OVEREEN	STEVE	P	1988
OVERMILLER	BOB	INF, OF	1969
OVERMIRE	FRANK (STUBBY)	MGR	1962-63
Major-League Debut:	1996 Montreal Expos		
OWEN	LUKE		1940
OWEN	TOMMY	C	1991
PABALIS	DON	INF	1944, 1947
PACHECO	ALEX	P	1992-1993
PAEPKE	JACK	MGR	1957
Major-League Debut:	1961 Pittsburgh Pirates		
PAFFEL	BOB		1955
PAGEE	SHAWN	C	1994
PANICKO	DON		1954
PAPARELLA	JERRY		1955
PAREDES	JESUS	INF	1987-88

LAST NAME	FIRST NAME	POSITION	YEAR(S) IN JAMESTOWN
PARKHURST	LYLE	P	1942, 1944-45
PARRISH	LARRY	OF	1972
Major-League Debut:	1974 Montreal Expos		
PARTYKA	JIM	P, OF	1968-69
PASCOE	TOM	P	1946
PASTER	DICK	OF	1969
PAUL	RICHARD	P	1943
PAXTON	DARRIN	P	1991
PEARCE	RON	P	1978
PECKHAM	PETER	P	1970
PEDRAZA	RODNEY		1991
PEGUERO	FELIX	INF	1971-72
PEKICH	DAVE	OF	1965
PELOT	HOWARD	P	1945-46
PENANICK	AL		1954
PERCHAK	JOHN		1939
PEREZ	MARCOS	OF	1973
PETERS	DOUG	P	1964
PETERSON	MERLIN		1939
PETERSON	PAUL		1939
PETRO	PAUL	OF	1954
PETTINI	JOE	INF	1977
Major-League Debut:	1988 San Francisco Giants		
PHELPS	THOMAS	P	1993
PHILLIPS	DICK	OF	1977
PHILLIPS	JACK	MGR	1964
Major-League Debut:	1947 N. Y. Yankees		
PHILLIPS	SAM	P	1968
PHILLIPS	TONY	INF	1978
Major-League Debut:	1982 Oakland A's		
PIECHOTA	JOE	INF	1979
PIECHOWSKI	TIM	OF	1988
PINION	EARL	P	1943
PINKHAM		C	1950
PIPIK	GARY	OF	1989
PISCIOTTA	SCOTT	P	1992

LAST NAME	FIRST NAME	POSITION	YEAR(S) IN JAMESTOWN
PITKO	MIKE	P	1966
PLASKETT	ELMO	C	1957
Major-League Debut:	1962 Pittsburgh Pirates		
PLITT	CHARLES		1942
PODEIN	GEORGE		1939
POLASEK	JOHN	P	1990
POLLACK	CHRIS	P	1987
POLLOCK	JOHN	C	1939, 1941, 1946
PONTE	ORVILLE		1956
PORTER	WILLIAM		1941
POTES	TOM	C	1953
POVLICK	GENE	P	1968-69
POWELL	HOWIE	INF	1954
POWERS	MIKE	P	1981
PRATT	HAROLD	P	1943
PRICE	BOB	P	1950
PRICE	JAMES	P	1943
PRICE	JOSEPH		1939
PRIEBOY	ANDY	P	1948-49
PSVTKA	HARRY	C	1949
PUJAIS	DARIO	P	1944
PURVIS	MIKE	OF	1966
QUADE	SCOTT	INF	1993
QUALLS	JERRY	INF	1964
QUEEN	JESSIE	OF	1956
QUINONES	RENE	INF	1980
RADER	GEORGE		1944
RALIEGH	MATT	INF	1992-93
RAMIREZ		P	1987
RAMOS	RICK	P	1978
RAMSEY	KEN	P	1966
RAPP	EARL		1941
Major-League Debut:	1949 Detroit Tigers		
RATLIFF	DAN	P	1982-83
REAGANS	JAVAN		1988

LAST NAME	FIRST NAME	POSITION	YEAR(S) IN JAMESTOWN
REDMOND	WAYNE	OF	1965
Major-League Debut:	1965 Detroit Tigers		
REECE	BOB	C	1973
Major-League Debut:	1978 Montreal Expos		
REED	MARK	P	1979
REGAN	PHIL	P	1956
Major-League Debut:	1960 Detroit Tigers		
REGIRA	GARY	P	1989
REITNOUR	RAY	C	1948
RENKENBERGER	HOWIE	INF	1965
RESPONDER	MARK	P	1993
RESSLER	RICHARD		1940
RHINE		C	1973
RICHARDS	GREG	P	1983
RICKER	TROY	INF, OF, P	1986-87, 1990
RIETSCH	LOUIS		1940
RILEY		INF	1971
RISCH	GEORGE	OF	1954
RISLEY	GEORGE	P	1952
RIVERA	ANGEL	P	1988
RIVERA	JESUS (BOMBO)	OF	1971
Major-League Debut:	1975 Montreal Expos		
RIVERA	HECTOR	C	1982
RIZZO	CHARLIE	INF	1984
ROBERTS	DAVID	OF	1994
ROBERTS	JEFF	C	1978
ROBERTS	JIM	P	1966
ROBERTSON	OTTO		1942
ROBERTSON	STAN	OF	1992
ROBITAILLE	MARTIN	INF, COACH	1988, 1992
ROBLES	AQUILINO	C	1984
ROCHEVOT	FRANK	P	1943
ROCKWEILOR	DEAN	P	1986
RODGER	BOB	OF	1956
RODRIGUEZ	ABBEY	INF	1990
RODRIGUEZ	ANTONIA	INF	1970

LAST NAME	FIRST NAME	POSITION	YEAR(S) IN JAMESTOWN
RODRIGUEZ	BUENAVENTURA	1B	1989
RODRIQUEZ	BOI	INF	1987
ROE	MICHAEL		1982
ROEDER	STEVE	INF, P	1979-1980
ROEHNER	MARK		1982
ROENICKE	GARY	INF	1973
Major-League Debut:	1976 Montreal Expos		
ROGALLA	STAN	P	1941-1942
ROJAS	LARRY HILARIO	INF	1962
ROOKER	JIM	OF	1961
Major-League Debut:	1968 Detroit Tigers		
ROONEY	PAT	OF	1978
Major-League Debut:	1981 Montreal Expos		
ROOT	MITCH	INF	1994
ROSADO	MANNY		1983
ROSE	KENNETH	OF	1950
ROTHE	WALTER	INF	1971
ROTHROCK	KERMIT	P	1944
ROY	JACK	P	1982
ROZMAN	RONALD	P	1951
RUBIN	HAROLD	P	1943
RUGGERIO	JOSEPH		1940
RUNDELS	MATT	INF	1992
RUPP	KEVIN	P	1977
RUSHWORTH	JIM	P	1992
RYAN	FRED		1961
SABATINI	JERRY	INF	1961
SACCOCIO	MICHAEL		1982-83
SADOWSKI	ED	MGR	1971
Major-League Debut:	1969 Boston Red Sox		
SAFFER	JONATHAN	OF	1993
SAJONIA	BRIAN	P	1988
SAMPLES	TODD	OF	1990
SANFORD	JACK	INF, MGR	1943
SANTANGELO	FRANK	INF	1989
Major-League Debut:	1995 Montreal Expos		

LAST NAME	FIRST NAME	POSITION	YEAR(S) IN JAMESTOWN
SARNA	TOM	INF	1953
SASS	TOM	OF	1942
SATTLER	BILL	P	1979
SAVAGE	AL	P	1943
SCHERUISH	MIKE	OF	1979
SCHMIDT	BOB	P	1962
SCHMIDT	CURTIS	P	1992
Major-League Debut:	1996 Montreal Expos		
SCHMIDT	RICHARD	P	1940-41, 1943-44
SCHNEIDER	THOMAS	P	1993
SCHRAMM	KEN	OF	1950
SCHROEDER	JOHN		1955
SCHROEDER	TOM	INF	1962
SCHUETT	JOHN		1954
SCHULER	MARK	P, COACH	1981, 1984
SCHULER	RONALD	C	1963
SCHULTE	MIKE	P	1982
SCHULTZ	JACK	OF	1948
SCHUPP	CHARLES		1942
SCOTT	ANTHONY	OF	1971
Major-League Debut:	1973 Montreal Expos		
SCOTT	CHARLES	P	1981
SELLECK	BOB	P	1966
SELTZ	ROLLAND (RICHARD)	INF	1943
SENZIG	JERRY	C	1961
SERLEY	EDWARD	P	1950
SHAFFER	DUANE	P	1940-41, 1944
SHANNON	BOB	P	1985-86
SHAW	BOB	P	1953
SHAWKEY	BOB	MGR	1950
Major-League Debut:	1913 Philadelphia A's		
SHEAFFER	JEFF	INF	1985
SHELTON	BOB	OF	1964
SHEPHARD	KELVIN	OF	1987-88
SHERER	WALLY	INF	1962-63
SHIFLETT	MATT	P	1987

LAST NAME	FIRST NAME	POSITION	YEAR(S) IN JAMESTOWN
SHIMP	TOM	P	1977-78
SHINES	ANTHONY (RAZOR)	INF	1978
Major-League Debut:	1983 Montreal Expos		
SHOOP	RON	P	1955
SHUPPER	FRANK		1944
SIDDALL	JOE	C	1988
Major-League Debut:	1993 Montreal Expos		
SIMMERS	JACK	P	1967
SIMMONS	MAX	P	1953
SIMMONS	WAYNE	INF	1979
SIMONONIS	ROBERT	P	1950
SIMONS	MITCH		1991
SIMS	JOE	OF, INF	1986-87
SINCLAIR	JOHN	OF	1970
SINTON	WILLIAM		1941
SIRRINE	ERNIE	C	1950
SITARZ	JOHN (JACK)	INF	1970
SKENDERIAN	TOM	OF	1968
SKIDGEL	JOHN		1939
SKORUBA	ELLIOTT	P	1981-82
SKULLEY	JOHN	P	1964
SLOAN	JIM	C	1980
SLOUGH	LESLIE	C	1970
SMALL	DON	OF	1970
SMALL	MIKE	P	1965
SMALL	ROBERT	C	1989
SMITH	CANNON	INF	1972
SMITH	DAN	OF	1973
SMITH	ELMER		1948
SMITH	GARY	P	1969
SMITH	GENE	INF	1965
SMITH	GEORGE	P	1943
SMITH	LEROY	P	1965
SMITH	RICK	C	1983-84
SMITH	RONALD	P	1943
SMREKAR	FRANK	P	1940-41

LAST NAME	FIRST NAME	POSITION	YEAR(S) IN JAMESTOWN
SNYDER	PAUL	P	1945-46
SNYDER	RONALD	C	1946
SOCRATES	ANTHONY		1943
SOLAREK	CARL	C	1965
SOLARTE	JOSE		1988
SOMA	CAS	P	1983
SOMMER	DAVE	P	1989
SOUTH	MARK	P	1978
SOUTHARD	FLOYD	C	1943
SPADOLA	FRANCIS	INF	1970
SPARKMAN	PAUL	P	1968
SPENCE	JACK	P	1973
SPENCER	GERALD	P	1970
SPORN	MORRIS	P	1943
SPROVIERO	NICK	P	1991
SPYHALSKI	JIM		1956
ST. CLAIRE	RANDY	P	1979, 1981
Major-League Debut:	1984 Montreal Expos		
ST. CLAIRE	STEVE	OF	1986
STACHEIT	GLEN	OF	1982
STAFFON	GREG	P	1977
STAIRS	MATTHEW	INF	1989
Major-League Debut:	1992 Montreal Expos		
STANLEY	KENNETH	OF	1950
STANLEY	TIM	INF	1988
STANTON	SNAKE	P	1983
STAUFFACHER	STUART	P	1985
STEELE	MIKE	P	1992
STEENKEN	MARK	C	1977
STEFFEE	KEITH	P	1944
STEINMETZ	MARK	INF	1977-78
STENNETT	FERNANDO	INF	1973
STEPHEN	JOHN	OF	1969
STEWART	BOB	INF	1956
STOH		INF, OF, C	1945
STONE	ED (BUD)	INF	1950

LAST NAME	FIRST NAME	POSITION	YEAR(S) IN JAMESTOWN
STREET	BILL (GABBY)	OF	1950
STRICKLAND	DONALD M.	OF	1949-50
STULL	EVERETT	P	1992
STUMP	JIM	P	1951
Major-League Debut:	1957 Detroit Tigers		
STUTTS	DENNIS	P	1993
SUBERVILLE	AL		1942
SUCHAN	CURT	OF	1968-69
SULLIVAN	PAUL	P	1968-69
SUNDGREN	SCOTT	P	1985
SUTHERLAND	JOSEPH A.		1944
SUTPHEN	GEORGE	OF	1945
SWANSEEN	HENNING		1939
SWANSON	CHIPS	P	1967
SWANSON	ROBERT		1941-42
SWANZAY	LARRY	INF	1985
SZABO	ROBERT	OF	1951-52
SZAJKO	DAN	INF	1982
TABAKA	JEFF	P	1986
Major-League Debut:	1994 Pittsburgh Pirates		
TABONE	LOUIS	P	1941
TACKITT	GLEN	P	1972
TARUTIS	PETE	P	1991
TAYLOR	AL	P	1953-54
TAYLOR	BOB	INF	1953
TAYLOR	CHARLES		1939
TAYLOR	JEFF	P	1978-79
TAYLOR	MEL	OF	1978
TAYLOR	STAFFORD	OF	1950
TEJADA	ALEJANDRO	INF	1989
TESSIER	LAWRENCE D.	P	1949
TESTA	NICK	COACH	1978
THIESSEN	TIM	INF	1982
THODEN	JOHN	P	1989
THOMPSON	ANGELO	OF	1993
THOMPSON	RHETT	INF	1966

LAST NAME	FIRST NAME	POSITION	YEAR(S) IN JAMESTOWN
THOMPSON	YOUNG H.	P	1951
THORNTON	EARL	P	1973
TICCONY		C	1947
TINDALL	MARK	P	1983-84
TINSLEY	KEITH	P	1971
TOBIAS	GRAYLING	OF	1978
TOMASSO	VICTOR		1941
TOMKINS	EARL	OF	1966
TORRES	CECILO		1945
TORRICELLI	TIM	MGR	1993
TOSOME	JOE	OF	1993
TOSTENSON	RON	OF	1984
TOVAR	EDGAR	INF	1992
TRAEN	TOM	P	1983
TRAKAN	VINCE	P	1953
TRAMMELL	THOMAS (BUBBA)	OF	1994
TRAVELS	DARRON	P	1986
TREADWAY	STAN	INF	1977
TREMBA	MIKE	OF	1977-78
TROSIN	ALVIN	P	1948
TRUMBULL	RANDY	P	1978
TRUSKOWSKI	AL	P	1968-69
TSCHOPP	MARK	P	1972
TSITOVRIS	MARK	INF	1990
TUCK	GARY	C	1978
TUHOLSKI	JIM	P	1964
TURNER	BRANDON	P	1990
UHLE	GEORGE	P	1944
VACCARO	SAL	P	1986
VAIANA	JIM	C	1979
VALDEZ	SERGIO	P	1984
VALENZUALA	RAY	INF, OF	1971
VALLIANT	BOB	P	1982
VAN DERZEE	RICHARD H.	P	1949-50
VAN REMMEN	TOMMY	P	1954
VAN WAINA	JOHNNY		1943

LAST NAME	FIRST NAME	POSITION	YEAR(S) IN JAMESTOWN
VANDERWAL	JOHN	OF	1987
Major-League Debut:	1991 Montreal Expos		
VANRYN	BEN	P	1991
Major-League Debut:	1996 California Angels		
VANWICKHAM	JOHN	P	1943
VATZKA	JOHN		1941
Veal	Coot	INF	1952
Major-League Debut:	1958 Detroit Tigers		
VENABLE	JOHN	P	1955
VENN	TOMMY	P, C	1940
VERSTRAETE	WHITEY		1956
VETTER	ROBERT	P	1943, 1945
VIEFHAUS	RANDY	INF	1972
VILTZ	COREY	OF	1987
VIOLA	JOHN	OF	1954
VITERETTO	PETE	OF	1953
VOGT	EARL		1940
VOSS	GENE	P	1965
VOTH	DOUGLAS		1940
WALKER	JOHN	INF	1977
WALKER	LARRY	INF	1985
WALROD	CHET		1939
WALTERS	DICK		1956
WALTERS	GEORGE		1954
WALTERS	KEN	OF, INF	1952-53
Major-League Debut:	1960 Philadelphia Phillies		
WARD	FRANK	P	1969
WARD	ROGER	P	1969-70
WATKINS	BOB	P	1977
WATKINS	DAVE	C	1963
Major-League Debut:	1969 Philadelphia Phillies		
WATKINS	KEN	P	1970
WATSON	ART		1939
WAYMIRE	RON	P	1982
WEATHERFORD	BOB	P	1977
WEBBER	FREDERICK		1940

LAST NAME	FIRST NAME	POSITION	YEAR(S) IN JAMESTOWN
WEBER	NEIL	P	1993
WEDVICK	JEFF	C	1986-87
WEGNER	FRED	OF	1970
WEINSHREIDER	ELMER	INF	1942
WEISLAK	KEN	INF	1980
WELAJ	WALTER		1940
WELBORN	FRANK	P	1986
WELCH	EDWARD	P	1939
WELLS	ROBERT	INF	1994
WERNER	CHARLES		1940
WERNER	DAVID	P	1948
WERNER	DON	MGR	1989
Major-League Debut:	1975 Cincinnati Reds		
WESSEL	TROY	P	1989
WEST	JIM	INF, C	1972
WESTRAY	KEN	P	1980
WHITE	CURTIS	P	1962
WHITE	DERRICK	INF	1991
Major-League Debut:	1993 Montreal Expos		
WHITE	JOHN	OF	1991
WHITE	MAC	OF	1994
WHITE	LOREN	C	1985
WHITE	RON	P	1969
WHITEFIELD	JEROME	INF	1980
WHITEHEAD	DENNIS	C	1973
WHITEHEAD	STEVEN	P	1989
WHITEHOUSE	JACK	INF	1963
WHITSON	EDWARD (NED)	P	1943
WICK	JACK		1940
WICKS	DICK	P	1967
WIEGHAUS	TOM	C	1978
Major-League Debut:	1981 Montreal Expos		
WIGLE	BILL	P	1946
WILAND	JACK	COACH	1986
WILKINSON	TODD	OF	1984
WILLIAMS	DICK	P	1964

LAST NAME	FIRST NAME	POSITION	YEAR(S) IN JAMESTOWN
WILLIAMS	JOHN		1941
WILLIAMS	RICK	P	1977
WILLIS	JOHN	P	1978
WILSON	HARRY	P	1947
WILSTEAD	RANDY	INF	1990
WINSTON	DARRIN	P	1988
WINTERS	HARRY	INF	1944
WIRTH	EDGAR W.	P	1949
WISKUP	PAUL	P	1939
WITUCKI	RONALD	C	1952-54
WOHLER	VINCENT	OF	1950
WOLFENBARGER	KENT	INF	1968-69
WOOD	DUNCAN	P	1965
WOODS	TYRONE	INF	1989
WREN	FRANK	INF, COACH	1978, 1981-83
WRIGHT	BILL	P	1970
WRIGHT	JOHN	P	1969
WRIGHT	ROBERT	P	1962
WRIGHT	ROBERT W.	C	1949
WRIGHT	WALLY	INF	1972
WYATT	JOHN	OF	1966
WYBERANEC	TED	INF, P	1942, 1946-47
WYNNE	JIM	P	1991
YANNI	VICTOR	INF	1944
YENSER	STEVE	P	1981
YERA	CECELIO		1945
YONKMAN	LEN	P	1972
YOUNG	BLAINE	P	1968
YOUNG	BRYAN (PETE)	P	1989
YOUNG	ROY	INF	1956
YUHAS	MIKE	P	1977
ZABALA	PETE	INF	1969
ZALOCHA	GEORGE	OF	1964
ZBEROOT	JOHN	C	1970
ZELENAK	NICHOLAS	INF	1961
ZIMMERMAN	GEORGE	C	1942
ZUCCARO	RICO	OF	1964

INDEX

BIBLIOGRAPHICAL NOTE

The vast majority of source material for this book came from the *Jamestown Post, Jamestown Evening Journal, Jamestown Post-Journal,* and original interviews conducted by a tenacious research team led by Greg Peterson and Russ Diethrick.

Most statistics were gathered from two primary sources: *Total Baseball IV: The Official Encyclopedia of Major League Baseball* and the *1994 New York-Penn League Guidebook.*

Other texts which served as background material include: *Good Enough to Dream,* by Roger Kahn; *Baseball: An Illustrated History,* by Geoffrey C. Ward and Ken Burns; *Baseball Weekly 1993 Almanac,* by Paul White; *Baseball America's Directory* (1992-1996); *The Minors,* by Neil J. Sullivan; *Only the Ball was White,* by Robert Peterson; *Chautauqua Lake Hotels,* by Helen G. Ebersole; *Jamestown and Chautauqua Lake Trolleys,* by Harold J. Ahlstrom; *The Negro Leagues Book,* edited by Dick Clark and Larry Lester; *The Negro Leagues,* by David Craft; *Saga from the Hills,* by M. Lorimer Moe; *Aaron to Zuverink,* by Rich Marazzi and Len Fiorito; *Aaron to Zipfel,* by Rich Marazzi and Len Fiorito; and *The Celoron Acme Colored Giants* (article), by Greg Peterson.